A Person of Purpose

A Person of Purpose

LESSONS IN LIFE FROM GOD'S PEOPLE

Alistair Begg
Stephen Gaukroger
Elizabeth McQuoid

11 10 09 08 07 06 05 7 6 5 4 3 2 1

First published 2005 by Keswick Ministries and Authentic Media
9 Holdom Avenue, Bletchley, Milton Keynes, Bucks, MK1 1QR, UK
and 129 Mobilization Drive, Waynesboro, GA 30830-4575, USA
www.authenticmedia.co.uk

British Library Cataloguing in Publication Data
A catalogue record for this book is available from the British Library

ISBN 1-85078-642-9

Cover design Sam Redwood
Print Management by Adare Carwin
Printed in the UK by Haynes, Sparkford, Yeovil

Contents

The aim of this study guide vii

PART ONE

Introduction 3

Chapter 1: Three funerals and a famine 8

Chapter 2: Unless God intervenes 16

Chapter 3: Homeward bound 26

Chapter 4: A momentous decision 37

Chapter 5: A divine coincidence 47

Chapter 6: Grace and favour 56

Chapter 7: An audacious plan 68

Chapter 8: Cold feet and redemption 77

Chapter 9: An old sandal and a new wife 88

Chapter 10: The mystery of history 99

PART TWO

Introduction 109

Chapter 11: Elijah – God's prophet on the run 110

Chapter 12: Samson – Passion and power out of control 122

Chapter 13: Deborah – A woman of courage and conviction 135

Chapter 14: David – A man after God's own heart 149

Chapter 15: Joshua – The crossover man 163

THE AIM OF THIS STUDY GUIDE

The aim of this study guide is to help bridge the gap between the Bible world and our own. Alistair Begg retells the story of Ruth and then Stephen Gaukroger looks at the lives of Elijah, Samson, Deborah, David and Joshua, great heroes of the faith. Both speakers explain that God works his purposes out through the ordinariness of people's lives. The stories of these Bible characters remind us that God still wants to use individuals to shape his world, change his church and to bless community and society. The questions that follow help relate the principles the speakers draw out to our own lives and situations. You can use this guide either for your own devotional time with God or with a group. Enjoy your study!

USING THIS BOOK FOR PERSONAL STUDY

Begin by praying and reading through the passage and commentary a number of times before looking at the questions. You may find it helpful to note down your answers to the questions and any other thoughts you may have. Putting pen to paper will help you think through the issues and how they specifically apply to your own situation. It will also be encouraging to look back over all that God has been teaching you.

Talk about what you're learning with a friend. Pray together that you'll be able to apply all these new lessons to your life.

USING THIS BOOK IN SMALL GROUPS

In preparation for the study, pray and read the passage of Scripture and commentary over a number of times. Use other resource material, such as a Bible dictionary or atlas, if they would be helpful. Each week, think through what materials you need for the study – a flip chart, pens and paper, other Bible translations, worship tapes?

At the top of each chapter we have stated the aim. This is the heart of the passage and the truth you want your group to take away with them. With this in mind, decide which questions and activities you should spend most time on. Add questions that would be helpful to your group or particular church situation.

Before people come, encourage them to read the passage and commentary that you will be studying that week.

Make sure you leave time at the end of the study for people to 'Reflect and Respond' so they are able to apply what they are learning to their own situation.

PART ONE

Introduction

Ruth is arguably one of the finest short stories that can be found anywhere in literature, biblical or beyond. Someone has said that no poet has written a more beautiful short story. Those of you who write at all would be struck by the wonderful symmetry and the way in which this story unfolds.

The world of eleventh and twelfth century BC Palestine is a very different world from the urban settings in which many of us live our lives. One of the challenges for us is to think ourselves back into the framework of the text. Before we delve into the details of the story, it's important for us to, first of all, try and get the big picture. It's important when we read our Bibles, for example the Old Testament narrative, that we don't read it in a truncated way that simply stops and starts, because it wasn't written in that way. It was written as an unfolding story. I want to encourage you, as it were, to squeeze your eyes as you look at the text and tell me what you see. You will discover, for example, that the opening and the closing of the Book of Ruth gives us some help in getting a handle on what the story is about.

Notice that the account begins in the days when the judges ruled. When you turn to chapter 4 you realise that, purposefully, it concludes with a genealogy and the final individual in it is King David. The strategic place that he has in history is there for us.

Let's begin where the text begins. 'In the days when the judges ruled' – that gives us not only the time period, but it also indicates the cultural and the theological and the moral climate in which this little story is set. You don't have to be a student of the Book of Judges, you need only to give it a cursory glance, to realise that the story of

Judges is a story that is absolutely frightful. Both socially and religiously, it is chaotic.

Hubbard, the Old Testament commentator, says that 'the book of Judges teams violent invasions, apostate religion, unchecked lawlessness and tribal civil war.' Even allowing for hyperbole, that is quite a thought. The story of Judges is the story of the Israelites living in the Promised Land after the death of Joshua. Instead of heeding the words of warning that God had given through both Moses and Joshua, they rebel against God's rule. Judges chapter 2 verse 10 explains, 'After that whole generation had been gathered to their fathers, another generation grew up, who knew neither the LORD nor what he had done for Israel. Then the Israelites did evil in the eyes of the LORD and served the Baals'. The story goes on and then in verse 16: 'Then the LORD raised up judges, who saved them out of the hands of these raiders. Yet they would not listen to their judges but prostituted themselves to other gods and worshipped them. Unlike their fathers, they quickly turned from the way in which their fathers had walked, the way of obedience to the LORD's commands.' Verse 19, 'When the judge died' (the one that God had raised up) 'the people returned to ways even more corrupt than those of their fathers, following other gods and serving and worshipping them. They refused to give up their evil practices and stubborn ways.'

The whole story makes depressing reading and by the time you reach the concluding chapters, from about 17 on, the brutality and the immorality have become commonplace; at least equal to our contemporary newspaper headlines. Look at chapter 19 verse 22. There's a man who comes into the town square, he doesn't have anywhere to stay, a kindly fellow offers him hospitality, takes him to his home, feeds his donkeys, washes his feet and, after they've had a cup of tea, verse 22, a great hullabaloo begins outside.

> While they were enjoying themselves (that's the little group in the house), some of the wicked men of the city surrounded the house. Pounding on the door, they shouted to the old man who owned the house, 'Bring out the man who came to your house so we can have sex with him.'
>
> The owner of the house went outside and said to them, 'No, my friends, don't be so vile. Since this man is my guest, don't do this disgraceful thing. Look, here is my virgin daughter, and his concubine. I will bring them out to you now, and you can use them and do to them whatever you wish. But to this man, don't do such a disgraceful thing.'

That's the moral, religious, theological climate which is concluded in Chapter 21:25, with the hint that there is a way to get out of this. 'In those days, Israel had no king; everyone did as he saw fit.' So as the story of Judges ends, there is the hint that everything would much better in the lives of God's people, if they had a king and, as it turns out, it would be really much better if they had a king who was after God's own heart. And who was the king who was to fit that description? David was to fit that description. And where do we find David introduced to us, as the final word? In the final verse of the fourth chapter of Ruth.

I stay there purposefully to make this obvious point. Notice that Ruth begins in the days when the judges rule. What time are we talking about, what was it like? The camera is about to get very, very focused on this little village. What was going on around the village? As the Book of Judges ends, the night, if you like, has become chilly, it has become dark and it is closing in on people. And the inevitable question that the child of God would be asking is 'Where in the world are we supposed to find a ray of hope in the midst of all of this chaos?'

Unless I am missing something, that's increasingly the word that I hear from the people of God. Having read the morning newspapers, having watched the broadcasts, having reflected on the moral, social, theological climate of Great Britain, the people of God, as I listen to them, are saying, 'Where in the world is there a ray of light in the midst of all of this chaos?'

Edersheim describes the Book of Ruth as a 'summer's morning after a night of wild tempest'. We have all had that experience, of going to bed at night with a storm beating and blowing on us, then to awaken in the morning and into all of the darkness and the chill of the previous night has come the splendour of the sunshine. That's essentially what we have in this story. In the lives of ordinary people, going about their routine daily chores, the work of the Lord continues unabated.

In one sense, that's why Ruth is here. It's here for more than that but it is here to say to the people of God, 'Listen, even though it may be dark all around, even though it may seem to be completely chaotic, look at what God is doing.' We are tempted to look to the Establishment for the answer, we look there and turn away with disappointment. That may be because God wants us not to look there but to look into the cottages, the high streets, the back streets, the council schemes, the places where ordinary people live out their routine days under the hand of God.

The book of Ruth takes our gaze off the heroes. There are no judges here, no Samson, no Gideon, no Jephthah, no amazing story of Rahab. In fact, when you read it, you say, 'Who are any of these people, and why does Naomi get such a big part? Who's Naomi? Why is it always Naomi this, Naomi that, Naomi the next thing? I thought it was called Ruth? It's as though God is preoccupied with Naomi.'

Actually God is preoccupied with people like Naomi. God, in the midst of everything that unfolds in life, in the mystery of his purposes, sets his love and affection on unlikely people, in unlikely contexts, doing routine things. This story is about how God is the God of the ordinary.

CHAPTER 1

Three funerals and a famine

Aim: To learn how to remain obedient to God during difficult times

FOCUS ON THE THEME

Whatever age and stage of life we're at, however long we've been Christians for, we have all experienced difficulties; times when, to a greater or lesser extent, we felt our lives were falling apart. If it is appropriate, share one of these occasions with the group. Explain what happened, how you felt and what you learnt about God and yourself through the experience.

Read: Ruth 1:1-5

If the Book of Ruth is, as Hubbard says, like a 'summer's morning' then we are forced to say that, on the strength of these first five verses, the day started out very cloudy. I've given this opening study the title, 'Three funerals and a famine', because here we find life falling apart in the space of five verses. How quickly lives can fall apart. With the result of a blood-test, the loss of a loved one, a decision made, perhaps rashly, in a moment of time – how quickly life can unravel. Certainly that is clear in these verses. And at the very heart of the decision-making process is the factor of a famine in the land.

The writer doesn't tell us how the famine came about. God had warned his people that famine would be one of the results of their failure to obey his commands carefully. You will find that at the end of Deuteronomy. 'If you don't obey me,' he said, 'I will come and I will punish you', and one of the mechanisms was famine. It could be simply a result of the invasion of enemy forces. It could be a result of drought. But it is a result of the providential dealing of God. And it is this famine which provides the backdrop, introducing us to this little family of four. 'There was a famine in the land and a man ...'

Those of you who know your Bibles may find that just the mention of famine rings bells for you. 'There was a famine in the land', remember, and Abraham went down to Egypt to live there. 'There was a famine in the land' and Isaac went to Abimelech, the king of the Philistines. Wasn't it on account of a famine in the land that Jacob and his sons ended up in Egypt? In each case, the famine proved to be pivotal, a turning point in the lives of the people of God, as it was in the life of the young man in Jesus' story in Luke 15. That is no surprise, in light of the drama of Scripture and in light of Jesus' knowledge of the Old Testament. When people heard the word 'famine', they knew that it often had proved to be a moment of great historical significance. Jesus says 'There was a severe famine in that whole country, and he began to be in need. So he went and hired himself out to a citizen of that country, who sent him to his fields to feed pigs.' The ears of the listeners are up again, 'Oh, you mean the way it happened with Abraham, a famine is significant, the way it happened with Naomi and her husband? Is this the story, Jesus?' The famine proved crucial.

- *'In each case, the famine proved to be pivotal, a turning point in the lives of the people of God.' What circumstances, people or events in recent history do you think God has used to help shape the direction of the church?*

- *List the top five things God regularly uses to shape you and bring you back to obedience. It could be the weekly sermon, the influence of your spouse or a particular circumstance, for example.*
- *Why does God allow hardship in our lives? Brainstorm as many reasons as you can.*

To everybody else reading their newspapers, it was just 'We're down on our crops' or 'It's exceptionally rainy' or 'We're having a difficult time' or 'The interest rate is drastic' or 'The housing market is escalating.' Through it all, the child of God knows not to look there, not to the city of London, not to the parliamentary structures but to recognise in the very details of history that God is working things out according to the eternal counsel of his will. And in each case of famine, not least of all here, his servants were protected and provided for.

- *How can we ensure that our response to hardship is different to that of our non-Christian contemporaries? What practices, habits or outlook do we need to put in place?*
- *If it is appropriate, share with the group a present concern or issue where you need to remind yourself that, even though it may not seem like it, 'God is working things out according to the eternal counsel of his will.'*

The reader is keen to find out, 'What happens to this little family?' 'There was a famine in the land, and a man from Bethlehem in Judah, together with his wife and two sons' ... made a decision. Bethlehem was about the same distance from Jerusalem as Grasmere is from Keswick. Bethlehem nestled in the foothills of Judah and had those same fields where later David, before he became king, as a shepherd boy would tend the flocks. Bethlehem is set in the same Judean hillsides where the angels would come and announce to the shepherds good tidings of great joy for all people. Bethlehem, ironically, means 'house of bread.' Bethlehem is not living up to its name.

Try to imagine Elimelech and his wife lying in bed before sleep finally takes them. And they're lying there, reflecting on things and they converse with one another. Elimelech asks his wife's advice. He says to her before they fall asleep, 'What do you think we ought to do?' Then he answers his own question, 'We could leave.' She says, 'What would people say?' He says, 'They can say what they like. If they could leave they probably would leave. But we have to think about the boys, their friends, uprooting them, taking them away.' Naomi says, 'Elimelech, what do you think God wants us to do?' Elimelech says, 'He wants us to use our brains. He wants us to be discriminating. He wants us to lean on our understanding.' Naomi says, 'Don't you think it might be good, if we trusted in the Lord with all our hearts and trusted him with this famine and didn't rely on our own insight? After all, he can give plenty or little. Why don't we trust him to direct our paths?' Elimelech says, 'I'm going to sleep.' He rolls over, pulls the blankets up, gets up in the morning and makes the announcement, 'We're leaving, we're moving.' Look at what he says, 'We're not going to live there for ever, we're only going to live there for a while.' 'With his wife and his sons he went to live for a while in the country of Moab' and it was going to prove just for a while but not in the way that he thought.

The author doesn't pronounce any judgement on this. Some of us are going to criticise Elimelech immediately and say this was very bad of him to do. From one perspective it was very understandable; he's supposed to provide for his family. The extremity of the circumstances is real. The opportunity for him to move is clear. But from another perspective, it is absolutely astonishing. Here he is in 'the house of bread', his name is 'Elimelech' which means 'My LORD is king', he knows that the blessing of God is directly related to the place of God and that God's people are to be in God's place if they are going to live under God's rule and God's blessing. He also knows that the people of Moab are on the list of those with whom the people of God should not associate. So he knows he is in the place of bread, he knows that God is faithful, he knows that his name means 'the LORD is king', he knows that his boys are going to say 'If the LORD is king, why are we leaving?' and yet still he gets up and he goes. All of us, if we are honest, have made decisions in our lives and then, upon reflection, have said, 'Maybe if I had the chance again, I would actually do that differently.' But the wonderful thing is that through it all and over it all, God remains in control.

- *Making decisions during times of hardship is often difficult. As a group, come up with a list of principles for how we can make God-honouring decisions.*
- *Consider the following scenarios. What advice would you give to these people who have decisions to make and are keen to remain obedient to God?*
  - *A couple feel God wants them to be missionaries but they are unsure which country God wants them to serve in or which organisation to be affiliated to. How should they proceed?*
  - *A family is wondering whether to change churches. Their main concern is that there are not many other families in their church and little is offered for their three sons. They are unsure whether to remain and try to help in their present church or join a more flourishing one for the sake of the children.*

- *A group of church leaders are praying about whether they should plant a new congregation in another part of town or whether they should build a larger auditorium for the growing number of people who attend the Sunday services. What factors do they need to think through and what action should they take?*

- *What difference does it make to you to know that even though we may regret decisions we have made, God always remains in control?*

It's plain that they were unable to leave without causing a stir. It's not as if they could just slip out. I take that because when we get to the end of the chapter and Naomi and Ruth come back, they arrive and the whole town is stirred. If the whole town is stirred by the two women coming back, I can assume that it was probably stirred on the way out. There seems to be a suggestion that this family was an important family. This Ephrathite business seems to be almost the indication of clan involvement. This is like the McGregors from Pitlochry moving to some wild place like England and it causing a huge stir. That's the significance of the Ephrathites from Bethlehem, they may actually be among the more resourceful of those from Bethlehem. When Naomi reflects upon things upon her return, she says, 'I went out full.' She had the fullness of her family and that has gone but there was probably a little more to it than that. It's certainly true to life because it's expensive to move. When things are very, very depressed economically, not everybody is able to move and most people can only hunker down and wait for the end of the famine. Yet Elimelech was able to make decisions. He made the decision and he moves his family out.

The fact that these verses are so full of these names indicates the importance of what is going on here. As we'll see as the story unfolds, they carry special significance in the purpose of God. Elimelech, 'my LORD is king': that's interesting, given your approach, Elimelech. Naomi, this lady whose name means, 'lovely' or 'pleasant' or 'delightful'; it's significant that we learn that name in light of all the bitterness that she experiences. And these boys, Mahlon or Kilion; I can't imagine that anyone has called their children Mahlon or Kilion since but I'm sure some have. They will be disappointed to discover that their names were from two Hebrew words that sound very much like 'Sickly' and 'Pining'. Although Elimelech, in the process, fails to live up to his name, God remains true to his covenant promises because there is no shadow of turning with God.

All of that is there in these opening verses. Remember 'Everything that was written in the past' says Paul in Romans 15:4 'was written to teach us, so that through endurance and the encouragement of the Scriptures we might have hope.' There is nothing in the Bible that is extraneous to us. This is all important stuff.

- *How have you been encouraged or challenged by these verses from the book of Ruth?*

FURTHER STUDY

'The blessing of God is directly related to the place of God and God's people are to be in God's place if they are going to live under God's rule and God's blessing'. Where is 'the place of God' and how has the meaning of this phrase changed through time? Scan through the Old Testament – where was 'the place of God' for Moses, David and Solomon? What would Daniel have learnt about 'the place of God' during the exile? Is there a physical 'place of God' in the New Testament? How would Paul have described 'God's place' – see Ephesians 3:12, Philippians 2:1, Colossians 2:6-7, 9-12 for example. How does the phrase 'the place of God' apply to you today?

REFLECTION AND RESPONSE

Consider your personal history.

- Spend time reflecting on the decisions you have made in the past, both good and bad. Accept the truth that although you may wish you had done things differently God is still in control.
- Remember the lessons that God has taught you through past hardships and put them into practice.

Consider your present circumstances.

- What is God trying to teach you?
- How are you seeking to remain obedient to him?

Consider your future plans.

- Remember God uses even physical realities such as a lack of resources, moving house and being a parent to teach us to be more obedient to him.
- Be assured that although the future is uncertain, God promises to be faithful to you and your family.

In twos, pray about the particular hardships you are facing. Commit to being obedient to God and trust his faithfulness during these difficult times.

CHAPTER 2

Unless God intervenes

Aim: To understand and share God's compassion for individuals

FOCUS ON THE THEME

When we have a project to do many of us have a 'get the job done' mentality and we imagine that God must be like that too. But the book of Ruth reminds us that even though God cares for the whole world he has a special concern and compassion for individuals. Share with the group a time that was particularly meaningful because someone took an interest in you as an individual. What did they do that was so special and why did it make such an impact on you?

Read: Ruth 1:1-5

In the course of verses 3 to 5 we discover that, although the family was to find the food they so desperately required, they were also to face circumstances which were dreadfully painful. In the space of just these three verses, you have a funeral followed by two weddings followed by two funerals. No details are given, just the bald facts. Elimelech dies and Naomi is left with her two sons. That's bad enough but things were to become even more distressing. Notice that the camera is on Naomi a lot. Usually if you read your Bible carefully, you will find that the women are introduced in light of the men. Here the man is introduced in light of his wife; he is described as the husband of Naomi. It's interesting and it's purposeful. Naomi is left not only without her husband but she is then left without her two sons. Of course they had married and the marriages held the happy prospect of children coming along but not only were there no children born, now the potential fathers were dead as well. As a result of that, the family name and the family's future was over. And the importance of the name for posterity's sake is at the very heart of the culture of the people of God and at the very heart of this little story. 'It is a bad thing that I have lost my husband, it is a worse thing that I have lost my sons because now I am in a situation where our name has found itself in a cul-de-sac and I am now absolutely hopeless and I am bereft.'

You have a lonely widow living as an alien in a foreign place minus the protection and provision of a husband, in a male-dominated society. Some of you are widowed and you have been for a long time. The people come, the people go, the day opens, the day continues, the day ends, it is like that. Decisions made in the past, events of history have brought you to where you are today. Life is hard and lonely and you may feel like Naomi, hopeless and bereft.

Naomi, widowed, faced the prospect of her declining years with no sons to care for her, no grandchildren to distract her and really very little to cheer her spirits. Walking out in the neighbourhood she catches a reflection of her face in a pond and looks down at herself and says 'Oh, Mrs Pleasant, Oh Mrs Delightful, what has happened to you? You're not so delightful now, are you, Naomi? You're not really the way you wanted to be. Your family name is extinguished unless God intervenes.' Then she probably said under her breath, 'Fat chance!' Driven from her homeland by famine, cruelly robbed of her loved ones by death, a lonely old widow sits abandoned in a foreign land. That's what we're told. The focus of God is on a sad and lonely lady. Remember what's going on in the culture. While this lady lives out her life within the framework of her routine, regular life continues all around her. For herself, she is facing her own personal dilemma. 'Forget the world and all that stuff in the public square', she says. 'I don't have time, I don't have emotion for that. I have my own problems. No husband, no sons, no grandchildren. I have my daughters-in-law, they're nice girls, but they're still my daughters-in-law.'

- *Recall what was happening to the Israelites during the time of the Judges and at this point in their history in particular. How does this make God's focus on Naomi all the more remarkable?*

Isn't it amazing that God gives a whole book to the domestic history of a woman? It's the only book in Bible that is given over to the domestic story of a lady. It's fantastic. It shows the amazing compassion and empathy of God for the backstreets and side alleys and the people who feel themselves to be last, lost and left out. God says, 'No, the whole world is going on, but I'm with you. I hem you in behind and before. I have set my hand upon you.' That's the kind of God we worship.

- *Many believers would agree with the phrase 'You're not really the way you wanted to be.' What is Christianity's answer to those who share Naomi's hurt that life hasn't turned out the way they'd hoped?*
- *In what ways do you and your church show God's compassion to 'the last, lost and left out' in society?*

If she'd had the privilege of living after William Cowper, Naomi would have occasion to retreat to the hymn that is familiar to many of us. She would have grabbed to herself the stanza, 'Judge not the LORD by feeble strength but trust him for his grace; behind a frowning providence he hides a smiling face.' All that she had to go on was that. But that's enough.

When you look at this lady and the drama unfolds, you realise that her view of the world remains fixed on the God of Abraham, Isaac and Jacob. She doesn't regard herself as being held in the grip of some kind of blind impersonal force. You are not going to find her singing to herself '*Que sera sera*.' She won't be doing that. She feels that she's losing 10-0 and there's only four minutes to go before the final whistle but it's not '*Que sera sera*.' Nor does she view her life as if she were a cork, bobbing around on the ocean of chance. She would have had no time for the kind of existentialism that is pervasive in our culture, 'It doesn't matter, whatever's going to happen is going to happen. Life is a short journey. It's a dirty trick. It goes from nothingness to nothingness.' She would not have been happy with Sartre in his book, *Nausea*, when the character Quentin goes out into the community and walks in the park and as he ponders the futility and meaninglessness of life, reflects to himself 'Every existence is born without reason, prolongs itself out of weakness and dies by chance.'

In the streets of Keswick, on the pavements of Liverpool, on the buses of Glasgow and in the undergrounds of London, we rub shoulders with the population that has come to believe this notion that 'I was born by chance, my DNA got introduced to itself in a slimy pool, I am a result of time plus matter plus chance. Therefore I'll do what I want, when I want with whoever I want, while I can, because after all, when you're dead you're dead and that's all there is to it. This is a short journey of aimlessness.'

Why is suicide amongst teenagers so high? Why are the university students that take their own lives the brightest?

They are not the people who are about to fail, they are the people who are about to excel. But they have been told, 'This is your life' and they've said to themselves, 'If this is it, it's a pointless existence.'

- *Consider how what you believe about the meaning of life affects your attitudes and treatment of individuals. If you believe in existentialism, that life is pointless and everything happens by chance, what will this mean for how you treat individuals? Give practical examples. If you believe in God and that he controls and gives meaning to life, how should that affect how you treat individuals?*
- *As Christians, how can we grow in our compassion for individuals?*

But not for Naomi. Naomi would have been a Westminster Confession girl. She would have gone to question number 11 in the Shorter Catechism and to the question 'What are God's works of providence?' she would have replied, 'God's works of providence are his most holy, wise and powerful preserving and governing of all his creatures and all their actions.' Or with Berkhoff, 'God's providence is the continued exercise of the divine energy whereby the Creator preserves all his creatures, is operative in all that comes to pass in the world and directs all things to their appointed end.'

In a way that was intensely personal, Naomi had to grapple with this. What she was going to discover and what she has now discovered from the vantage point of eternity is that God was doing something far bigger than anything she could ever see. If you like, the story before us is a wonderful exposition of Romans 8:28. 'And we know that in all things God works for the good of those who love him, who have been called according to his purpose.'

What is the good that God is working towards? It is the separating out of a people and the transforming of a people into the likeness of his Son. He does use famine. He does use failure. He does use the silly, obviously bad things that we do, in order ultimately to accomplish his final strategy for us. In your peculiar circumstance in life where the world crashes around you, don't forget that God is the God of the ordinary.

- *What comfort or encouragement is there in knowing that your life fits into a much larger plan of God and that he does have a strategy and goal in mind for you as an individual?*

Let me finish with a warning and an encouragement. The warning is the warning of James chapter 4, because some of us are very 'Elimelechal' in our approach to things. To those of us who are ready to make rash decisions, James says

> Now, listen, you who say, 'Today or tomorrow we'll go to this or that city, spend a year there, carry on business and make money.' Why, you do not even know what will happen tomorrow. What is your life? You are a mist that appears for a little while and then vanishes. Instead, you ought to say 'If it's the LORD's will, we will live and do this or that.' As it is, you boast and brag. All such boasting is evil (James 4:13-16).

If that had been the *Daily Bread* reading for Elimelech that morning, it might have been a help. Instead he said, 'We're going to Moab, but we're only going to be there a while. Boys, don't worry, we'll go down there and we'll be back.' They never came back.

All our decisions are significant. And the thing that stabilises the believer is to be reminded that in it all and through it all, God is at work and that is finally the encouragement that we derive from this, reminding ourselves that God is the God of our ordinary lives. The 'Who' and the 'Where' and the 'What' and the 'When' of our days are all issues that are held in his hands.

- *Why are we so often reluctant to bring the ordinary, everyday concerns of life to God?*
- *Think about the 'Who', 'Where', 'What' and 'When' of your life. Take a few minutes to write a question against each of these words which explains your present concerns and anxieties.*
  – Who?
  – Where?
  – What?
  – When?
  For example, 'Who can I ask for help when my partner is away on business?' 'Where should I apply for a new job?', 'What can I do now my children have left home?', 'When will I get married?'
  Consider what it means that all of your concerns and questions are held in God's hands.

'Aren't two sparrows sold for a penny and yet not one of them will fall to the ground apart from the will of your Father', Jesus says. 'So don't be afraid, you're worth more than many sparrows.' Look at yourself in the mirror. This morning the hotel receptionist said, 'If you require a rubber bathmat, ring the front desk.' I thought about it for just a moment. I've never thought about that in my life. I looked at my face in the mirror. 'You're frightened you will slip in the bath?' 'Yes.' You look at yourself as gravity takes hold, as you disintegrate before your very eyes, as you can't find your car keys or your car in the car park and you don't recognise your children on the other side of the street, and you say, 'I'm not worth tuppence.' Jesus says, 'You're worth more than a couple of sparrows.'

- *What does God think of us? On a large piece of paper or flip chart, brainstorm your ideas and find quotes from the Bible describing what God thinks of us. A good place to start could be Psalm 103:13-14, Isaiah 62:5 and 1 Peter 2:9-10.*

Finally, these opening verses serve as an antidote to the notion that the path of faith is strewn with rose petals. Neither the Bible nor human experience encourages us to think in that way. Yet one of the reasons, possibly, that we fail to make the impact we could in a culture that is increasingly disillusioned, disheartened and fearful, is because we have bought the idea that to declare ourselves to be members of the family of God, is almost to speak in terms of triumph, almost to speak in terms of 'We've got it together.'

I can't imagine how many people, who feel themselves to be ordinary and left out, would gravitate towards many of our congregations. They come in and they say, 'These people don't understand, these people are all fine, apparently. They just sing and everything's fine.' Of course we want to be triumphant and declare the glory of God but we have to be prepared to get real with people and tell them, 'You know, I'm a lonely widow and my husband's been dead for forty years and I still cry' or 'I'm a single mother and every so often a sense of regret and bitterness overwhelms me to the point of distraction' or 'I'm a father who made a bad decision which God has swept into his will but that decision confronts me always and everywhere.' People will say 'I didn't know that faith could be like that.'

- *What impact do you think it would have on the church community and unbelievers if Christians were real and expressed their weaknesses, hurts and limitations? How can we make the church a safe place for this to happen?*
- *Look back over Ruth 1:1-5 and the commentary in this chapter. What hope and truth are offered to those of us who feel very ordinary and weak individuals?*

FURTHER STUDY

The Bible gives us other examples of women who have trusted God through difficult circumstances. Look for example at the lives of Hannah (1 Sam. 1:1– 2:11) and Anna (Lk. 2:36-38). What do we learn about God from these accounts? What lessons do we learn about what our attitudes and actions should be during hardships?

REFLECTION AND RESPONSE

In silence, write down on a piece of paper a list of the bad decisions you've made, the times you've failed, and the hurts you have suffered. If you have not done so before, ask God's forgiveness for any wrong actions and attitudes. Then, rather than dwelling on these issues any longer, commit them to God, trusting him to work all things out according to his will. Write over your list in bold letters the answer to question number 11 in the Shorter Catechism, 'God's works of providence are his most holy, wise and powerful preserving and governing of all his creatures and all their actions' and Romans 8:28, 'And we know that in all things God works for the good of those who love him, who have been called according to his purpose.'

As a group, spend time praising God for his care and compassion. Thank him for his intimate concern for the details of your life, for his faithfulness towards you and his work in your life.

REVIEW OF RUTH 1:1-5

The Book of Ruth opens with a series of crises. There is moral decay and a political crisis as the judges repeatedly deliver the Israelites from their enemies and try to secure civil peace. There is an economic crisis when famine hits, and there is a personal crisis in Naomi's family when her husband and two sons die, leaving her without any security or support. These first five verses paint a hopeless picture and pose the question 'What will God do?'

Many of us can identify with Naomi and know what it feels like when the world seems to collapse around us. If you are going through a difficult time at the moment, acknowledge your need for God and ask 'What will God do?' Look forward with anticipation to his answer and don't be surprised to find him working in the most unexpected ways.

Perhaps your life is going well at the moment but that should not stop you asking the question, 'What will God do?' Pray through the activities you're involved in and the various relationships you have. Are you expecting God to work? Or have you ordered your life so well that you don't really need him? Ask God to show you areas of your life you need to surrender to him and be willing to take action.

POINTS TO PONDER

- What have you learnt about God?
- What have you learnt about yourself?
- What actions or attitudes do you need to change as a result?

CHAPTER 3

Homeward bound

Aim: To appreciate both the joys and the struggles of the Christian life

FOCUS ON THE THEME

In this chapter we see that hardships and difficulties are not mistakes or aberrations but part of the life of faith for all believers. The good and the bad days, the hellos and goodbyes, the laughter and the tears are all woven into God's purpose for our lives. Think back over the times you have met someone you haven't seen for a long time and the occasions you have had to say goodbye to a loved one. Share with each other your happiest 'hello' and your saddest 'goodbye'.

Read: Ruth 1:6-22

We have seen already in the first few verses of the book of Ruth that God is at work in the events of ordinary lives. Naomi's experience of life and of God remind me of a paragraph from the very brief biography of the late Fred Mitchell, *Climbing on Track*. He was the director of the China Inland Mission, a frequent speaker at the Keswick Convention and member of the Council in the 1940s. The biographer, at one point in the opening section of the book, says this

> He accomplished no great thing, his name was linked with many Christian organisations but he was the founder of none, he made no spectacular and inspiring sacrifices, he effected no reforms. This is the story of an ordinary man from a village home with working class parents, who spent the greater part of his life as a chemist in the provinces and who, on that ordinary humdrum track, walked with God.

He died along with others in a plane crash in India on the 2nd of May 1953 and people mourned his passing in the same way as Naomi mourned the passing of her husband and her sons.

We ended our last study by suggesting that it was at least worthy of consideration that one of the reasons for our less-than-effective impact on our culture lies in our determination to put a brave face on everything. The triumphalistic ramblings of Christians grate upon the ears of the tender-hearted and broken-hearted. It is a striking feature of this opening chapter of Ruth that Naomi attempts no such thing. The way in which she describes the misfortune that has come her way, the source of that misfortune as the hand of the Lord going out against her, and her honesty that although her name means 'pleasant' her life is bitter, is an antidote to the temptation to try and import heaven into the now. Eventually, one day we will be freed from the very presence of sin but in the interim we live seeking the Spirit's enabling over the power of sin and dealing with the ravages and the implications of life in a foreign world.

Atkinson, in his most helpful commentary on Ruth, has so many wonderful pictures it's hard not to steal them all. Some of you, familiar with that work, will be able to identify them and if some slip in without my acknowledgement it is not a desire to be involved in plagiarism, it's simply that I began to imagine my scribbles as my own. But one of the wonderful pictures he uses of faith is that faith is not a still light, but it is a mobile; the things that we hang in our children's or grandchildren's bedrooms with all the bits and pieces that move around. He says when you hang one of these things in a room, at times, one of the characters or one of the pieces will be in the shadows and then, as it moves around, it will come into the sunshine. That, he says, is the life of faith for the believer. He goes on to say that Naomi is an illustration of the fact that if we're honest about our lives, some of our pains seem unbearable, some of our circumstances seem so unjust and some of our questions, indeed through all of our lives, will remain unanswered.

- *What other illustration could you use to give a new Christian an honest assessment of what to expect from the life of faith? How could you prepare them for the hardships that God allows and the times when he seems far away without dampening their enthusiasm for their new journey of faith?*
- *Why do we have difficulty accepting that hardship, struggle and tragedy are part of the life of faith and not aberrations to be ignored or explained away?*
- *How would you respond to someone who said, 'What is the point of being a Christian if God does not relieve your pain or speak when you cry out to him in need?'*

Naomi testifies to that in a very simple and straightforward fashion. This lady, living as an alien in a foreign place, was obviously keeping in touch with her homeland. In this respect she's a bit like Nehemiah who was constantly hearing news as it was fed to him in Susa. The two of them, in very different contexts, would be all ears for news from home. If you've lived as an ex-patriot, beyond these fair shores, you will know how much it means when you're travelling and you hear on the radio, 'This is the BBC world service.' You want to take your radio and hug it. Naomi would have been like that. The news reaches her and she hears in Moab that the Lord had come to the aid of his people. Or, as one translation puts it, 'The LORD has visited his people.'

In this instance, he had come to the aid of his people by providing them with food. We shouldn't miss the simplicity of this statement. I constantly have to guard myself against taking things for granted, even the ordinary things in life. When you live in the world of Asda and Tesco or whatever your supermarket is, it is possible to start to forget that God is the Provider of everything that we have. He is the One who makes the rain fall, the sun shine and so on. That is why it is imperative for us to make sure that we don't get to the point in our Christian lives where saying grace is perfunctory. That is why it is a wonderful thing, as parents and grandparents, to make sure that our children and grandchildren are saying or singing their grace from the earliest of ages. I still have these wonderful recollections of my nieces in Glasgow singing together, 'Thank you for the world so sweet, thank you for the food we eat, thank you for the birds that sing, thank you God for everything'. I looked at those young girls, this past weekend, in Ohio and saw them growing into young teenagers and realised that the undergirdings of their teenage life had been largely framed and formed, not as a result of somebody sitting down and beating on them with information, but rather their parents nurturing them within the framework of God's provision and God's care.

Through the poor, painful tears of her disappointment, the sun shines in, the news comes and Naomi realises that Calvin was right when he said 'It is an absurd folly that miserable men take upon themselves to act without God when they cannot even speak except he wills.'

It is this wonderful news, the provision of food, that now reverses the outward journey and it's homeward bound for this trio. Naomi and her daughters-in-law prepare to return to Judah (verse 6). Naomi, in the company of these two girls, Orpah and Ruth, sets her course for home.

At some point along the road, when Naomi was presumably far enough away from Moab that she couldn't be encouraged to return, but not so far enough away to prevent her encouraging her daughters-in-law to return, this dialogue takes place. In verses 8-13 Naomi says 'goodbye' to her daughters-in-law and tries to persuade them to return to Moab.

Roger Whittaker, that whistling character of old, with the beard, had a song which had as a refrain, 'And the first time that we said "hello" began our last goodbye.' Goodbyes are important in our lives. Every goodbye is a preparation for our final goodbye when death will part us. We never know when our routine goodbye may prove to be our final goodbye. Therefore, the way in which we both greet people and part from people should be an evidence of our deep theological convictions. The English word 'goodbye' actually means 'God be with you.' We are saying in the awareness of our parting, that God is sovereign over all these affairs. As a family we often went to the north of Scotland on holiday, to little fishing villages way up on the north-east coast. The children from the village with whom we had bonded during the couple of weeks that we were there, would come through their back gardens and up the hill and the car would stop and there we would say 'goodbye' to one another. I would look out of the back window and long to be in the company of these boys and girls that I was leaving behind. Many of us have said goodbye to people who got on an ocean liner or an aeroplane and in some cases we never saw them again.

That is the context of this encounter. There are these three women and this is the dialogue that takes place. Incidentally, of the 85 verses in the book, fifty of them are dialogue; we are learning through conversations. What you have here is not a Kodak moment. This is a Kleenex moment. In a Kodak moment, people say, 'Does anybody have a camera?' A Kleenex moment is 'Does anybody have a tissue?' That's exactly what was necessary here. What a jumble of expectations, emotions, affirmations and misgivings is to be found in these events.

Some of the commentators, in fact quite a few, are convinced that Naomi was wrong to urge the girls to return to Moab. The suggestion is that she was concerned for herself and how she would look if she showed up back in Bethlehem with these two foreigners because it would highlight the fact that she had gone in the company of Elimelech and her boys and that not only had they been involved with the inhabitants of Moab but they had gone one step beyond that and had actually married inhabitants of Moab. So the commentators say that the reason that Naomi is urging the young women to go back home is promoted by self-interest.

Now you have to read your Bibles and figure things out, as I did, but I don't read the text like that. In fact, Naomi's urging here seems to me to be selfless. What has she got left in the world in terms of interpersonal relationships? These two girls; her husband's gone, her sons are gone and what little family she has left is here and she says, 'I think it is in your best interests to do this.' Notice her terminology in verse 8, 'May the LORD show kindness to you ... May the LORD grant each of you will find rest in the home of another husband'. Her concern for them is both prayerful and God-centred. She has in mind not her own well-being but their well-being and their security, a security that is ultimately found in Yahweh but is, in the immediacy, expressed in their mothers' homes and in a husband's embrace.

- *Consider the following scenarios. In what ways could you show a 'God-centred' concern for these individuals?*
  - *A couple have been members of your church for two years but complain to you that they still don't know many people or feel part of the fellowship.*
  - *The youth work in your church is going very well but the youth leaders mention to you that they are so involved with the ministry on Sundays and during the week that they feel isolated from the rest of the adult congregation and are missing the teaching.*
  - *A friend is struggling at work. He has an incompetent boss who shouldn't really have been promoted and whose workload he is carrying. Your friend wonders whether he should speak to his boss, speak to his supervisor or look for another job.*
- *Naomi's motives may have been questioned not just by commentators but by her contemporaries. We often struggle when people misinterpret our motives and actions. What God-centred ways have you found to deal with your own hurt and people's attitudes in these kind of circumstances?*
- *How does having a God-centred concern for other people's problems help us deal with our own struggles?*

A number of the books that I read (and I read quite a number in preparation for these studies) go like this, 'Naomi is a cantankerous old rascal, don't be like her. Ruth is a fine young lady, be like her.' I understand how the commentators come to this conclusion but I don't think its right. Look at Naomi here; this isn't a bitter old lady saying, 'Listen, if I can't get married, you're not getting married either. If this isn't going to work out well for me, I don't see why it should work out for you. The two of you,

you come with me. I'm Mrs Bitter, we're in this together to the bitter end.' She's not doing that. There is a selflessness about her and she commends them to the care and provision of God. 'May the LORD grant each of you this.' And she kissed them. In fact the phraseology that is used here in terms of the Lord's kindness is a word that you will have come across in your own studies; *hesed,* God's covenant love. She is commending them ultimately into the care of God. What else can we do for our children and those who are near and dear to us? The covenant love of God, says Alec Motyer, 'is that wonderful love that combines the warmth of God's fellowship with the security of God's faithfulness.'

- *What stops us wanting something better for others than we have ourselves? Why do we not pray God's* hesed *for others more often?*
- *What does our response reveal about us and our view of God?*

Picture this scene. Here you have these three ladies, all wrapped up in each other's arms, because presumably they are not standing seven or eight feet from one another. I think the three of them are a complete mess, all their mascara running, if they are wearing it, depending on what local church they were in, and their faces are just a snotty mess. Their noses are all red, the tissues are all in a tiny ball by this time; this is real life. This is what life is about. It's about hellos and goodbyes. It's about relationships. It's about how God Almighty interferes with our days, whom I marry and if I marry and all of these things are interwoven in the unfolding drama of God's purpose for our lives. All of these bits and pieces are the Christian life. Naomi urges them and she presumably thinks that she's prevailed upon them. 'Go back', she says. She hears them saying 'We will go back.' So she must have said 'Good.' And then they were saying 'We will go back with you and to your people.' 'Oh, no' says Naomi. 'No. Listen, wipe your eyes, blow your noses and try and be sensible for a moment.'

Then she gives this little speech there in verse 11 and the prolonged statement about 'What if I had a husband, what if I had one tonight, would you wait for the boys to be born?' It may sound strange to us but it will become apparent that she is referring to Levirate marriage. The essence of it is that if a man died childless, his brother had to marry the widow so as to produce heirs to continue the family line. Essentially, Naomi is saying there is no way it can happen. Even if she could have more sons and conceived tonight, Orpah and Ruth would be too old by the time the boys became men. Naomi's a little quick off the mark here. Apparently she was perfectly prepared to believe that God would be able to be king over the affairs of Orpah and Ruth, if they were to go back, even into alien territory. But when she thinks about her own circumstances, she can only see old age and loneliness beckoning.

It's quite fascinating. 'Now girls, this is what I want you to do. I want to commit you to the *hesed* love of God. He's wonderfully faithful and true. However, in my case, I've only got bitterness and loneliness.' So she says to them in verse 13, 'It is more bitter for me than for you.' She recognised that they had lost their husbands, they were not free from grief. But she says, 'It's more bitter for me than for you because the LORD's hand has gone out against me.'

Notice how her theology comes to the fore. She is not suggesting that the affairs of life are out of control. They are under God's sovereign control, in that he brings to pass all that he wills. Hubbard says, of this statement, 'Here we have bitter complaint cloaked in firm faith.' 'Providence' says one anonymous writer, 'is a soft pillow for anxious heads. It is an Anadin for pain. It is a grave in which to bury our despair.' As Naomi reflects upon her circumstances, she recognises that famine, exile, bereavement, childlessness have all proved to be in the will of God for her. And she affirms the fact that God is in control. There's no suggestion here of the contemporary regurgitation of an old heresy represented in open theism. But there is no suggestion here of Naomi saying, 'God turned his back and then everything went wrong' or 'God is as surprised by this as I am', which is a contemporary perspective that is gaining ever greater inroads in contemporary Christian thought here in the United Kingdom, and not least of all as a result of influential voices from across the Puddle. You need to learn to resist this thinking, firm in the faith. Naomi is a good reminder to us that God is too wise to make mistakes; he's too kind to be cruel.

- *'As Naomi reflects upon her circumstances, she recognises that famine, exile, bereavement, childlessness have all proved to be in the will of God for her.' As you reflect, what situations, events or sadnesses do you recognise have been in God's will for you?*
- *What have you learnt about your faith and about God through these difficulties?*

FURTHER STUDY

Look up the following Bible verses where the term *hesed* is used – Exodus 34:6, Deuteronomy 7:9, and Psalm 103:4. Also look up the term in a Bible dictionary (under 'loving kindness'). From what you have read, how would you describe the term *hesed*? What does God's *hesed* mean for us in practical terms, what did it lead him to do? What would it mean for us to show *hesed* to others and what change in our attitudes and actions would there need to be?

REFLECTION AND RESPONSE

Imagine your Christian life as a mobile. You may feel your life is in the shadow as you grieve, feel lonely or are ill. Perhaps your life is in the sunshine as you take part in family celebrations, use your spiritual gifts in a special way, or enjoy days of deep intimacy with God, for example.

Spend time in quiet reflection making an honest assessment of your spiritual life, your concerns and joys.

If it is appropriate, share your joys and struggles with another member of the group. Pray that each of you would recognise God's *hesed* in your life.

One day we won't struggle with sadness or hardships any more but we will enjoy heaven with God. As a group, meditate on Revelation 21:1-7 – pray and praise God for the home that he is preparing for us and that we are all homeward bound!

CHAPTER 4

A momentous decision

Aim:To assess the impact of our decision to follow Christ.

FOCUS ON THE THEME

The first chapter of the Book of Ruth is full of momentous decisions. In chapter 1:1-5 Elimelech decides to relocate the family to Moab and his sons decide to marry Moabite women. In 1:6-22 Naomi decides to return to Bethlehem, Orpah decides to return to Moab and most amazing of all, Ruth decides to accompany her mother-in-law back to Bethlehem, despite the uncertainty and lack of security she faces.

Share with the group a momentous decision you have made. It could be the decision to move house, to get married, or to change jobs, for example. Perhaps the most momentous decision you have ever made was your decision to follow Christ. Whatever your decision, you probably only realized its significance in hindsight. If it is appropriate, explain to the group the decision you made and how it has shaped your life subsequently.

Read: Ruth 1:6-22

When Naomi finishes her little speech, once again, it's tears. Verse 14: 'At this they wept again.' This little emotional triangle, or actually emotional quadrilateral because God is part of all of this, is there on the roadside. I'd love to know how long this went on, all this back and forth of tears, kissing and goodbyes.

Then the great divide comes. 'Then Orpah kissed her mother-in-law good-bye.' The kissing is changed now. She kissed them back in verse 9 and they responded 'We're going to stay with you.' She kissed them as a sign of closure, 'Give me a kiss, let's go.' They said, 'No, we're not going'; she gave the speech and Orpah said, 'You give me a kiss, I'm going.' Orpah kissed her mother-in-law goodbye. It's a defining moment, isn't it? Orpah has decided to be obedient. Orpah has made this sensible choice. What are we to make of this? Can we fault her for doing what Naomi has urged? Is she walking away from the Living God? Is this an illustration of a borrowed faith that she decides not to make her own in the moment of opportunity? Or is it possibly an illustration of someone who decides to return to alien territory to live under the shadow of Yahweh's protection? I don't know and neither do you.

One day, in heaven, we can say, 'Excuse me, has anybody seen Orpah? I was looking for Orpah because I don't know what happened on that roadway.' I don't know if she was saved. Wouldn't it be tremendous if Orpah's reasoning was, 'Naomi, you have convinced me so much that Yahweh is my Protector and my Provider that I will go back into the alien environment and under the shadow of his wings I will rest secure.' I'd love to think so, but certainly her response provides the velvet from the jewellers' store, if you like, on which the diamond, this remarkable statement of Ruth, is provided for us.

The cast is dwindling – there are only two left. Elimelech, Kilion and Mahlon, none of them had speaking parts. Then we have Orpah and Ruth, and a little bit said by Orpah, but nothing from Ruth so far. Naomi's doing all the talking and now there's only the two of them left. It's all about weeping and kissing and leaving and clinging. It's all very feminine, isn't it?

But maybe, men, we need to cry. I cry when I read the James Herriot books to my children. I recently read to them the story about the old horse down in the field and the farmer loved it so much that he didn't want to send it to the knacker's yard. My kids loved it and try to get me to read books just to see me cry. For some men, the reason they're all tied up is because they could do with a good weep, frankly. God gave us these emotions in order that they might be vehicles of release and expressions of what's going inside of us. These ladies, Naomi, Orpah and Ruth, are a wonderful example to us of what really is inside coming out.

In verse 16, Ruth makes her first statement in the book, and what an opening statement. She's had her last chance to change her mind, in verse 15. Orpah isn't quite round the bend yet, she's just beginning to get a bit distant but you can still see her, and Naomi says, 'She's not out of sight yet, you can still catch her. Go on, now. Make a run for it. I'm bitter, this is hopeless, there's no future. Go now while you've got the chance.' And what an amazing response Ruth gives. Where does this kind of response come from?

Ruth's eyes are following Orpah but her hands are clinging to Naomi. Ruth's heart is pulling her all over the place and her mind is formulating this little speech. One commentator says 'There is no more radical decision in all the memories of this realm.' Certainly, when you think about what this decision means in redemptive history, it's amazing.

> And Ruth said, 'Entreat me not to leave thee, or to return from following after thee: for whither thou goest, I will go; and where thou lodgest, I will lodge: thy people shall be my people, and thy God my God:

> Where thou diest, will I die, and there will I be buried: the LORD do so to me, and more also, if aught but death part thee and me' (Ruth 1:16-17: King James Version).

Summarised, she says to her mother-in-law, 'If you're going to put pressure on me, if you're going to entreat me, then put pressure on me not to leave you; don't put pressure on me to leave you.'

The fascinating thing to me is that the same fact that caused Orpah to return caused Ruth to stay. It was the same information that caused the decision. It was the absence of a husband for Naomi, or the presence of an heir or a son. Orpah processed the information and she decided that she would leave, desiring to become a wife. Ruth processed the information and decided that she would stay, committed to remain a daughter. The same circumstances, the same information, a momentous decision: 'Wherever you go, I'm there.' The commentator Hubbard writes, 'She took on the uncertain future as a widow in a land where she knew no one.' She wasn't going on a short-term missions project, was she? This was till death us do part. Even in death, she says, she will be buried with Naomi's people; that's a huge commitment.

- *The Holy Spirit plays a key role in drawing men and women to faith. But consider our generation – what is it about Christianity, Christians and our culture that influences people to make a decision for or against Christ?*
- *How has your commitment to Christ been challenged and tested since you made that initial decision to become a Christian?*
- *The decision to become a Christian is only the start of the story. How can we cultivate a 'till death do us part' kind of commitment to God? What role should the church, other Christians and we ourselves play in this process?*

In my early days of life in America, sometimes I woke up early in the morning and would think to myself, in a moment of panic, 'What if I die here? I can't die here. I can live here but I can't die here.' Maybe you have to be Scottish to understand that. I don't know, because coursing through your mind, you've got, 'As fair as fair as these green foreign hills may be, they are not the hills of home.' Frankly, one of the most salutary, staggering and impactful things for me in twenty-one years of living in the United States remains that issue.

- *The prospect of death challenges us to reassess our lives and priorities. How does it help you reassess your commitment to God? What concerns does it bring to light?*

When somebody says 'I'm with you through thick and thin, I'm committed to you. Where you go, I'll go. When you stop, I'll stop. What you do, I'll do. Whom you love, I will love. I'm with you not only to death but through death' – that's such a commitment. That's the commitment of a Jim Elliott who said, 'He is no fool who gives up what he cannot keep to gain what he cannot lose' and today his blood mingles with the Curaray River.

This commitment of Ruth's has proved to be a preachers' paradise, wrestled out of its context, pressed into sermons at marriages. It's not an illegitimate use, provided we pay attention to where it's set. And it is a wonderful illustration to us of what it means to be serious in our commitment to the Lord Jesus Christ.

- *What difference did the decision to follow God make in the lives of the first believers? Look at how Abraham, David and Paul depended on God and how they expressed a 'till death do us part' type of commitment to him. Genesis 22:1-19, 1 Samuel 26, Philippians 3:4b-14 might be helpful references to start with.*

- *How do the lives of these Bible characters encourage you or challenge your commitment to God?*

We used to sing, didn't we, as children 'I have decided to follow Jesus, no turning back.' Then that second verse, remember? 'Should no one join me, still I will follow, no turning back.' That's what she's doing here. Orpah is dear to Ruth presumably, and this is heart-rending. Ruth's statement means goodbye to Orpah, goodbye to familiarity, goodbye to everything that has represented security to her and hello to the great unknown. In the verses, it turns out, she has deep convictions about her decision to stay with Naomi, not only because of Naomi herself but also on account of Naomi's God.

- *Who or what have you had to leave or reject in order to follow Christ? Is there an extent to which following Christ is a lonely journey for you?*

Look at verse 18: 'When Naomi realised that Ruth was determined to go with her, she stopped urging her.' There's a turn in that verse in terms of interpersonal relationships. Naomi realised that she's won three sets and then, they just start walking but they're not talking. You can only hear their sandals on the sand.

Before they know it, they're round the bend and it's into Bethlehem. There's no possibility of slipping in quietly. It's quite remarkable that two widows could create such a stir. If you've experienced village life you will know that a sighting at one end of the street can become a birthday party at the far end of the street within about twenty minutes. That's village life and Naomi's return caused quite a buzz.

Women are nudging each other and saying 'Is that Naomi? She's looking old, isn't she? Do you think she's lost weight?' 'Where's her husband? What happened to the boys? Who's the girl she's with?' 'They say she's a daughter-in-law.' 'Really? I'm going to ask her.' So the lady went up to her and said 'Is this really you, Naomi?' And

Naomi replied, 'That's my name but it's not my experience. El-Shaddai has taken me down a bitter path. Full I went away, empty he has brought me back.'

Again, in this little dialogue, Naomi's honesty is striking. No hiding her feelings; no pretending about her life, no attempt to sweep it all aside with a stiff upper lip. Presumably walking into the town and seeing all the old familiar places brought back all kinds of memories. Maybe in the crowd, or in the bazaar, or in the market place, the quick-sighting of a friend who's grown old, the glimpse of young men who were contemporaries of her boys, the paths that she had walked on the early days with Elimelech, all of them combined to overwhelm her emotionally and she deals with her pain theologically. 'Oh God', she says, 'You are the Almighty One. Famine, bereavement, sadness, loneliness, yes. But you are the Almighty One, you are El-Shaddai. I can leave the explanations with you, the responsibilities with you.'

- *How does our attitude and thinking need to change for us to be able to stand back from our current situation and say, 'But you are the Almighty One, you are El-Shaddai. I can leave the explanations with you, the responsibilities with you.'*
- *What evidence has God given us throughout Bible history and in our present circumstances that our decision to trust him, even in difficult circumstances, is well-founded?*

Bethlehem is finally living up to its name. I was thinking of this story in film terms for some reason. I thought the background music in the early part of this film would have been a lament, certainly for the first five verses, a lone piper. But now, the sun is forcing its way through the clouds, it's shining through on the fields of barley, there's the inkling of a new day and the music changes and the lament goes and the melody line begins to pick up and more strings fill in the background. Because when God is at work, even hopelessness may prove the passageway to fresh starts and new opportunities. What chapter one eventually says to us is that he who is the King of the nations has the affairs of the world under his control. The Lord God omnipotent reigns. It may not always seem so but it is so and he who is King of the nations is also Lord of the ordinary. So don't miss the simple stuff; food on your table, companionship, tears, honest questions, and in it all the awareness that God is sustaining and guiding his children until, at last, the darkness is dispelled. Because, ultimately, the goodbyes of this chapter prepare us for the goodbye of death, and I am waiting for the dawning of the bright and blessed of days, when we will see Christ in all his fullness.

- *What does it mean for us that God is both King of the nations with the world under his control and also God of the ordinary? Brainstorm the practical implications of these twin truths.*
- *Despite your initial decision to follow God and despite knowing his greatness and care for you, what is holding you back from wholehearted commitment to him? What does God want you to do in light of this?*

FURTHER STUDY

Look at the following references where the term El-Shaddai is used – Genesis 17:1-2, 28:3, 48:3-4 and Exodus 6:3. What can we learn from these examples about the importance and significance of the term?

REFLECTION AND RESPONSE

Ruth's decision to follow Naomi's God had an impact on her immediate family, the community at Bethlehem and eventually, as we shall see, redemption history. Consider your own decision to follow Christ. It might have been a significant moment you can refer back to or it could be a process which happened over a number of years.

- How has your decision to follow Christ impacted your own life? For example, what have you left behind, what new relationships have you formed and what new priorities have you got?
- What impact has your decision to follow Christ had on your immediate family? Are they attracted to Christianity because of your behaviour and attitudes?
- How has your decision to follow Christ impacted your community? Is it a better place because you live there?
- How will your decision to follow Christ make an impact in history? How will subsequent generations describe the faithfulness of your service and devotion to God?

As a group, commit to God the areas your church is trying to make an impact in – the community projects, special services and outreach you are involved in. Commit both the big picture and the small details to God who rules the nations and is also God of the ordinary.

REVIEW OF RUTH 1:6-22

Reread Ruth 1:6-22. Imagine this first chapter is the opening scene to a film.

- God is the real hero in this story. What do we learn about him from this chapter?
- Consider the main characters in turn – Elimelech, Naomi, Ruth and Orpah. What have we learnt about them and their belief in God from their actions and conversations?
- If chapter 1 was the first fifteen minutes of a film, would you want to keep watching? If so, why? What are the clues in the text that something interesting is about to happen?

POINTS TO PONDER

- What have you learnt about God?
- What have you learnt about yourself?
- What actions or attitudes do you need to change as a result?

CHAPTER 5

A divine coincidence

Aim: To see our endeavours within the framework of God's providence

---

FOCUS ON THE THEME
Once in Bethlehem Ruth takes the initiative and goes gleaning in the barley fields. Although she is taking action, God is at work in the background and an apparent coincidence which will change the course of history has the stamp of God's providence all over it.

Describe to the group an event or circumstance in your own life which others would perhaps explain as coincidence but which you believe was God's providence at work.

Read: Ruth 2:1-3

It's no secret that I was born in Glasgow. It's something I'm very thankful for and quite proud of. Our home was adjacent to a secondary school in suburban Glasgow and when I was about eleven or twelve they put a large extension on the school. During the summer holidays, the school became a building site. Throughout the day the men that were working on the building site drank large quantities of lemonade and by the end of the working day, there were lemonade bottles all over the site. I would wait until I saw the last of the men leave and then I would go into the building site and work my way through it, picking up all the empty lemonade bottles and taking them across to one of the newsagents for a refund. I hope that wasn't dishonest, I don't think the men were planning on doing that. On a good day I could collect enough lemonade bottles to be able to get a round of golf at Deacon's Bank, which was the local public golf course.

All these years later I remember that with a measure of fondness and I recognise too that old habits die hard. Those who know me best will be able to testify to the fact that in the drive-through at a McDonalds Restaurant or any other restaurant that has a drive-through, it's not uncommon for me to get out of my car and pick up the change that other people have dropped. I assume that these people are either too wealthy or too lazy or too busy but I am none of the three and it gives me a tremendous measure of satisfaction to be able to pick up a clutch of coins and put them in my pocket.

I am fairly certain, based on what I've discovered here in Ruth chapter 2, that Ruth would have been very happy to commend me for my endeavours. She is involved in the equivalent of picking up lemonade bottles in this chapter. This is the evidence of subsistence living, the indication of what poverty was like in ancient Palestine. This young lady, having been transported from all that was familiar to her, wakes up on the first morning in her new home and, like anybody waking up on that new day, her heart and mind would be flooded with all kinds of things. It's not difficult for us to imagine her lying there, saying to herself, 'I wonder what's happened to Orpah? I wonder if she's back with her family now? Here I am, a widow. I'm living with my mother-in-law, also a widow. I'm an awful long way from my home. I'm an alien in a strange land. But you know, I've come to trust in Yahweh and he is my refuge. Probably life is going to be pretty ordinary and unexciting. There's no point in lying here just thinking about things. I need to get up and get on with the day.'

Before we follow Ruth through what is a day in her life, the narrator introduces us to a new character. The cast in this little play is about to become three again. And in this very intriguing and simple way, the author introduces us to this man, Boaz, by highlighting two things. First is the relationship that he enjoys with the clan of Elimelech. Again, this situation in Palestine was not dissimilar to life in Scotland in an earlier era, where families were identified with one another even though they might have different names because, ultimately, they could be traced to a common ancestor. Within that extended clan family there were relationships and there were expectations. That's what the narrator tells us here, that this man, Boaz, who was a relative on the side of Elimelech, was a man who had a relationship with Naomi. Also, he was a man of resources. That's the significance of the phrase that he was a man 'of standing' in verse 1. He's a man whose influence wasn't tied only to his financial resources, which were to become apparent, but also to his moral integrity. This man of standing intrigues the reader and we say, 'I wonder where he's going to reappear?'

Having introduced us to Boaz, the narrator picks up the story with Ruth. I imagine that village life in Bethlehem at harvest time would be fairly similar, in flavour at least, to harvest time in the north of Scotland. I remember, again, as a boy going north in Scotland and seeing tractors coming down a road with bags of potatoes on the back and people hanging off the back of the trailer with their legs dangling everywhere. The sights and sounds of harvest time pervaded the village. It was impossible to be there without being caught up in the immediacy of what was going on.

It was perhaps the very sights and sounds of the start of the barley harvest that stirred Ruth into action. We don't know when she formed the plan that now unfolds. We don't know whether she and Naomi, in walking towards Bethlehem and acknowledging their predicament and their poverty, perhaps began to converse with one another concerning the care that Yahweh takes for those who are poor. If they had that conversation, it obviously wasn't a theoretical one. What Ruth was to discover was that God's law, in keeping with his concern for the helpless, the poor and the sojourner, had long made provision for the needy.

For example, we read in Leviticus, 'When you reap your harvest, you shall not reap your field to its very border. Neither shall you gather the gleanings after your harvest.' God had made provision, in his law, for those who were poor and because God was concerned for the poor, he expected his people to be equally concerned. No matter how prosperous they were, they would treat individuals like Ruth and Naomi with a compassion which was representative of the compassion of God. There's nothing to be ashamed of in honest poverty. These two women were not poverty stricken as a result of indolence. They were not back in Bethlehem as a result of the fact that they had made poor choices and bad decisions and were lazy. They are commendable, particularly this young girl, Ruth.

So, in the morning Ruth said to Naomi, 'Let me go to the fields and pick up the leftover grain behind anyone in whose eyes I find favour.' In my notes, I simply collapse that to the phrase 'Let me go and find favour.' She's not looking at her mother-in-law and saying 'What am I supposed to do now?' or worse still, 'So what have you got planned for me, Naomi? This is where you live, I'm not from here, what am I supposed to do?' Nor does she suggest that it's time for Naomi to get up and get about the business. 'Come on Naomi, you're not dead yet. You might as well get out and do something.' No, instead she goes out on a limb. She risks being ostracized as a foreigner, perhaps even being harmed in the company of the workers. In this she provides a wonderful illustration of a principle that is increasingly absent in our culture: care for our elders. We need to care for those who have invested their lives in us, who nurtured us and who, in many cases, now find themselves living in abject poverty and, perhaps, in total isolation. Any of us who are tempted to give short shrift to the notion of honouring our fathers and mothers, and our extended parental responsibilities to aunts and uncles, can certainly derive no support from the example of Ruth.

The initiative here of Ruth is not only attractive but definitely instructive. Up in the morning, she's out to do what she can do. She knows that God will provide but she knows that God does not routinely provide in a vacuum. She knows that God is sovereign but she is coming to understand that his sovereignty takes into account her decisions and endeavours. She walks out into the morning aware of the fact that what she needs more than anything else is grace and favour. I can only imagine Naomi watching her as she goes off down the road and under her breath saying, 'Thank you, gracious God, for this wonderful daughter-in-law. So much common sense, amazing in her careful thoughtfulness and what a wonderful initiative she takes.'

- *What is there about Ruth's character that is 'not only attractive but definitely instructive'? Which of her qualities can and should we be modelling?*
- *If we are taking initiatives to provide for ourselves, how can we keep in mind that all we have is from God's hand? What practical measures can we take?*

- *Ruth found out that God provides but he does not routinely show his providence in a vacuum. Consider the following scenarios: what initiative do you think the individuals involved need to take and when should they be still and allow God to work on their behalf:*
  - *A couple needing to raise support to become missionaries.*
  - *A couple desperate to have a child but seemingly unable.*
  - *A church needing to raise money and find land for a new building.*
  - *A woman concerned about her family's finances and wondering whether she should go out to work.*
- *This chapter of Ruth in particular brings up the issue of caring for the poor and giving material resources to those in need. When is the last time you took the initiative and gave practical care to someone in need?*
- *God's providence in the lives of others often involves us in giving generously. What are the usual reasons that we give our finances and resources to Christian ministry? How does viewing our giving as God's instrument of providence alter your perspective?*
- *What are the issues for you in caring for elderly parents? If it is appropriate, share your concerns, difficulties and fears with the group.*

Verse 3, 'She went out and she began to glean in the fields behind the harvesters.' Who's field is she in? Boaz's field. What are the chances of that? There wasn't a big sign that said, 'Boaz' field', in fact it was a patchwork. And in the patchwork of a vast acreage, it would be divided up like allotments and everybody would have their little bits and pieces. The owners knew where they were but someone, as a routine stranger, wouldn't know where it was and so she just launches into the first place that she can. In the King James version verse 3 reads, 'Her hap was to light on a part of the field belonging to Boaz.' It just happened that way. She could have gone somewhere else but she went there.

- *Ruth turned out to be working in Boaz's field and in the course of the story he becomes increasingly central. How can we ensure that we are available to be used by God in his providence?*

Charles Simeon, in the eighteenth century, writing about the way in which the sovereignty of God and the freedom of human choice interface with one another, says 'What is before us? We know not whether we shall live or die but this we know, that all things are ordered and sure. Everything is ordered with an unerring wisdom and unbended love, by Thee O God, who art love.'

That perspective which, of course, doesn't answer all the questions about human choice and divine providential care is, at least, a pointer on the journey. And one of the things that it is important for us to hold on to is the fact that God overrules the freedom of our choices. For example in the life of Joseph, you have the same thing. Joseph's brothers were jealous because they were jealous. They were not jealous because God made them jealous, they were jealous because they were bad rascals and they were actually vindictively jealous. The Ishmaelite traders arrived at just the right moment as a result of the intervention of one of the brothers, so that they could, driven by a profit motive, pick up this remarkably handsome young Israeli boy and transport him off into captivity and sell him for a profit. The brothers were acting of their own volition. The Ishmaelites were acting on their own volition. And what was God doing? All of this, in the freedom of their choice, he was using according to the eternal counsel of his will to ensure that Joseph would be in Egypt to be able to provide for the very brothers who disdained him with jealous hatred. It is truly beyond our ability to comprehend. So what we should do is put our hands over our mouths and bow before God.

- *Is making the right choices and being involved in the most worthy endeavours more or less important to you if you believe that ultimately God will ensure his will and purpose happens?*

I was reading in the autobiography of F F Bruce, called *In Retrospect,*[1] on page 307. He makes a variety of passing statements and he says,

> For the Christian, this business of repeated choices and diminishing options, is bound up with the experience of divine guidance. Some of my friends can relate quite exceptional experiences of divine guidance. For myself, I have found it easier to trace divine guidance in retrospect than to recognise it at the time. But I must add, that the consciousness of free choice, has often been accompanied by a not incompatible sense of following a predetermined course. To commit one's way in advance to God especially but not only, when a momentous choice has to be made, is to have the assurance that one's way will be ordered, or overruled by God for good.

I found these thoughts very helpful and I hope that you do too and it may send you back to Bruce's biography itself, if you can find it.

- *As you look forward to all that the future holds, what security is there in committing your way to God? What does this mean in particular for your circumstances?*

FURTHER STUDY

Reread the story of Joseph in Genesis chapters 37 and 39-47 picking out all the examples of human choice being used by God in his providence. What do you learn about how God uses our good and bad choices and how his providence operates in the most unlikely of scenarios? Does Joseph's experience help you in any way to reconcile the idea of free choice operating alongside a sense of following a predetermined course?

REFLECTION AND RESPONSE

Consider God's work in your life:

- The times you have had dramatic experiences of his guidance.
- The times you have only seen his hand in retrospect.
- The times he has used others to show his providence.
- The times when you have taken the initiative but, as you took each step, you felt him ordering your way.

Consider the week ahead – the decisions and choices you will need to make and the endeavours you will be involved in. In twos, share with each other your concerns for the coming week and commit your way in advance to God. Praise God that you can rest secure that whatever happens your way this week will be ordered or overruled by God for good.

CHAPTER 6

Grace and favour

Aim: To recognise God's grace and favour and model it in our lives

FOCUS ON THE THEME
Boaz's grace and favour towards Ruth remind us of Jesus' kindness. Jesus intervened into our lives when we were destitute and without hope. His grace and favour were totally unmerited and we can only respond like Ruth in humility and gratitude.

When did you last show someone grace, treating them with more kindness and favour than they deserved? Or when did someone last show you grace – perhaps a boss allowing you extra time off for a particular reason, a spouse overlooking your criticism and responding with kindness, or a debt you owed being cancelled? Share your recent experiences of grace with the group.

Read: Ruth 2:4-23

In verse 4, the boss arrives. Some of you are aware of what it's like in your office, factory or lab when the boss arrives. Something happens: people start to shuffle, they get uncomfortable. But here, when the boss arrives, it's quite wonderful because Boaz arrives from Bethlehem with blessing on his lips. 'The LORD be with you' he said and

'The LORD bless you', they called back. What a wonderful place to work.

There's a lesson to be learned and we'll just deal with it in passing concerning employer/employee relationships. If you are a boss, you have a huge responsibility for the way in which you behave amongst your people. I was with a gentleman who's been retired now for seventeen years. He was the third generation to run a large contracting firm. I asked him, 'Do you miss it?' and he said 'I miss going on a building site at the time of the coffee break and sitting down and talking to the men and hearing how they're getting on and how their families are.' I suggest to you that he was probably a wonderful fellow to work for. He didn't say that he missed the sense of fulfilment but he missed the opportunity to hear from others. And the way in which we, as employees, respond on a daily basis is also of great significance. In fact, the way that we greet one another, the way that we say 'hello' and the way that we say 'goodbye' tells a great deal about us.

- *Whatever our role in life, whether we're an employer, employee, parent or ministry leader, we are responsible for our behaviour, using it to influence people for good and for God. In your particular context, what opportunities have there been to influence people by your behaviour?*

Boaz obviously knows his workers very well because, once we have identified him here as the boss, he immediately enquires what is going on. He asks the foreman of his harvesters 'Whose young woman is that?' Presumably he knew his group and therefore he would be able to identify the arrival of a new face. Perhaps she had a pretty face. I think we tend to think of Ruth as being very pretty but there is nothing that says she was. It's interesting that there is in most cases a complete absence of description in the Bible, not least of all in relation to the Lord Jesus himself, so that our focus might be on the right things.

The foreman gives a quite extensive answer to a very simple question. The question is 'Whose young woman is that?' and the foreman replies, first of all talking about her identity in verse 6, 'She is the Moabitess who came back from Moab with Naomi.' Then in verse 7 he talks about her humility, because she actually came and made a simple request 'I'd like to glean and gather among the sheaves.' He also mentions her industry 'She went into the field and she has actually worked steadily from morning till now, except for a while when she took a short rest in the shelter.' In other words, she is identified as quite a girl. She's living up to the expectation that was created when she told Naomi back in chapter 1 verse 16, 'Don't entreat me to leave you because I want to stay with you, I want to go with you, I want to be with you.' That level of commitment is not words, words, words. It is now translated into action and her action is revealed in the initiative that she takes, in the journey to Bethlehem that she makes, and in her commitment now to the hard task of gleaning. She is not simply a hearer of the great provision of God, she is a doer of things. She is on the right side of the exhortation of Paul when he writes to the Thessalonians in 1 Thessalonians. He tells them, 'Don't be a busybody, don't be a gossip. Make it your ambition to work hard, to keep your mouths shut and to get on with things.' That's a paraphrase, it's 1 Thessalonians chapter 4:11-12.

In light of the information he receives, Boaz then engages Ruth in conversation. Look at the tenderness with which he addresses her. 'My daughter' he says. This is the first indication of the age gap that exists between them. This is not a peer for Boaz, this is a younger lady. And he gives her this series of imperatives: number one 'Listen';

number two 'Don't go'; number three 'Stay here'; number four 'Watch'; number five 'Follow'; number six 'Drink'. It's good when you are reading the narrative to pick out these verbs because if you say 'What's happening here?' it's a succession of these statements. He introduces himself, he says, 'I don't what you to go anywhere else. I want you to stay here. I want you to watch the field where the men are harvesting. I want you to follow along with the girls. I have told the men not to touch you and, incidentally, if you are thirsty this is where you can get a drink of water, over there.' Ruth's response in verse 10 indicates the tenderness that must have marked his directives because she bowed with her face to the ground. I think we picture her falling on her knees and then bowing until her forehead touched the ground, a typical oriental gesture of humble submission to a superior.

What is she thinking? The writer tells us in the second half of verse 10; she exclaimed 'Why have I found such favour?' It's a matter of hours since she left in the morning. She asked Naomi if it would be all right if she went off and what was she going to do? 'Let me go and find favour.' Now she bows before this individual and she asks the right question, 'Why is it that I have found favour?' The hopes of the morning have been more than fulfilled. The circumstances were beyond what she could have asked or even imagined. We don't find her congratulating herself for her endeavours, saying to herself, 'This was a brilliant move on my part. I am really good. What a stroke of genius. How smart of me to pick out the right field.'

- *What prevents us recognising God's grace and favour in our lives?*

She knew that wasn't the case. It was 'her hap' that found her there. As it happened, she was there. Furthermore, she was a foreigner. When she thought about her life, she had worshipped foreign gods and she would still be worshipping foreign gods were it not for the intervention of the God of Abraham, Isaac and Jacob in her life through the decision, not necessarily a brilliant decision, of Elimelech to go where he really shouldn't have gone and to take his wife there. So, a bad decision produced a good result. It sounds like Joseph again. 'You intended it for harm but God intended it for good.' God sweeps even our silly mistakes into his unfolding purpose for our lives. We may rest content that nothing is out of control and so, as she reflects on this, and for the light that was shone into her darkness, it is thankfulness that expresses itself in her very posture. Thankful people are humble people and humble people are thankful people, and humility and thankfulness sleep in the same double bed. Her question ought to be the question on the lips of every believer, when we come before the One who has made provision for us and under whose protective custody we live; to come before Christ and say, 'Why have I found such favour?'

That's how Paul approaches it, for example, in Ephesians 2. It's a pattern not only in Ephesians – it's a Pauline pattern, constantly calling people to remember. He says

> Therefore, remember that formerly you who are Gentiles by birth and called 'uncircumcised' by those who call themselves 'the circumcision' (that done in the body by the hands of men) – remember that at that time you were separate from Christ, excluded from citizenship in Israel and foreigners to the covenants of the promise, without hope and without God in the world. But now in Christ Jesus you who once were far away have been brought near through the blood of Christ (Eph. 2:11-13).

- *What exactly is Paul urging us to remember? How does remembering keep us humble and thankful for God's grace?*
- *In what ways can we as individuals and a church follow Paul's command to remember? Brainstorm the many ways that remembering happens.*

In the sense that all of the Bible is about God and therefore about Jesus, it is surely not illegitimate for us to telescope our understanding of this and see Boaz pointing us forward to the great Provider, to the One who intervenes in the lives of those who are needy, poor, helpless and alone.

Boaz replies that her kindness to Naomi has not gone unnoticed. 'I have been told all about what you have done for your mother-in-law.' He doesn't say, 'I saw the sticker on the back of your little pack, you know.' He doesn't say, 'I heard your talk.' He said 'I heard all that you have done.' Let your light so shine before men that they may see your good deeds and glorify your Father who is in heaven. I have seen what you have done. I have heard of your kindness. Kindness – is that part of the fruit of the Spirit? I think it is.

Long after mental brilliance is forgotten, long after human eloquence is dispatched into the darkness of time, kindness will be remembered. Kindness is an undervalued grace. It is wonderful to be in the company of kindness and kindness ought to be a hallmark of the covenant love of God, expressed in his children. Talk is cheap in comparison to the expression of a love that is taken hold. 'Why would you be so gracious to me, a foreigner?' 'I've heard of your kindness.'

- *If kindness is a fruit of the Spirit, how do we cultivate it?*

Ruth is starting to look like her Father and so Boaz prays for her, verse 12, 'May the LORD repay you for what you have done. May you be richly rewarded by the LORD, the

God of Israel, under whose wings you have come to take refuge.' Isn't this what the writer to the Hebrews essentially says in Hebrews 6, 'God is not unjust, he will not forget your work and the love you have shown him as you have helped his people and continue to help them.' The distinguishing feature of Ruth's life was that her refuge was in Yahweh.

Verse 13, 'May I continue to find favour in your eyes, my lord.' Her circumstances were uncomfortable and notice, 'You have given me comfort and spoken kindly'. She faced the possibility of antagonism and she was brought under the jurisdiction of his protection. And she was amazed by this; such comfort, such kindness that he had shown her. Especially as 'I do not have the standing of one of your servant girls.' She is so far from thinking of entitlement. She regards the intervention of Boaz as an act of unmerited goodness, which it was. It was an act of unmerited favour. She is there with no standing, brought into the protection and provision of a man of standing, who is prepared to give her all that she needs and more.

Jesus is our man of standing, able to give us all we need and more. The Bible points us to him. In the Old Testament, Jesus is expected; in the gospels, Jesus is revealed; in the Acts, Jesus is preached; in the Epistles, Jesus is explained and in the book of Revelation, Jesus is anticipated.

Look at verse 14 and at the wonderful way in which Boaz treats her at mealtime. First of all his invitation to her is gracious: when she sat down with the harvesters, he offered her some roasted grain. But prior to that he had said, 'Come over here. Have some bread and dip it in the wine vinegar.' How kind of him and how generous now to offer her this roasted grain, to provide her with (notice verse 14b), all that she wanted and with some left over to take home.

- *Reread chapter 2 picking out all the ways that Boaz reminds you of Jesus. What does Boaz say and do that is Christlike?*
- *Boaz gives Ruth commands which she accepts with grateful thanks: indeed she interprets them as evidence of his grace. Why do so many people today assume that a God who gives commands is incompatible with a God of grace?*
- *How do God's commands show his grace and favour to you?*

Boaz, in operating in this way, operates graciously. He intervenes generously and his intervention crosses economic, social and racial barriers. She was poverty stricken, she had no standing at all. He was a prosperous man, he had his fields and he had his resources. She was a foreigner, they were divided racially from one another. She was without status, he was a man of standing. His intervention in her life crosses all of these barriers.

We could spend the remainder of our time talking about the way in which the gospel crosses barriers and we could work through every example of this but let me just address one.

A couple of days ago, one of your morning newspapers indicated the fact that 90 per cent of whites have few or no black friends. That, I would imagine, is not unique to secular society. It is more than adequately representative of the Christian church. Before we give ourselves a dreadful pain in the neck thinking about it, let us be as sensible as we can. The United States of America still suffers from the legacy of racial discrimination. Sixty years on, all that was represented in the hatred and vilification of black people in America still has implications. This is, in large measure, due to a complete misunderstanding or a complete misstatement of the Bible's teaching prohibiting intermarriage. People in an earlier generation said that God prohibited intermarriage on a racial basis. No, he did not. He prohibited the intermarrying with other people on a theological basis. For example, in

Deuteronomy 7 he tells his people 'I don't want you to intermarry with them, not because they come from a different culture, not because their skin is a different colour, not because they have a perspective of life that is different from your own but because they would turn your sons from following me to serve other gods.' That was the reason.

The issue was theological not racial, and the first principle on which the Christian discussion of the question of race is built is that as far as humankind is concerned, there is only one group. That's what Paul is saying in Acts 17, when he preaches to the Athenians. He says 'From one man came all of humanity on the face of God's earth. There is only one group. And membership in God's family is on account of grace, not race.' There is no priority ever given to race. The priority of God for the people of God extends even beyond the nation of Israel, out into a company that no man can number, that comes from every nation, tribe, language, people and tongue, creating the great vision of Revelation 7. 'And there' says John, 'I saw this group that no one could number and they came from everywhere.' Yet the fact of the matter is that I'm not sure that this intervention of Boaz, that crosses these barriers, is represented in any realistic sense at the present time, certainly not where I come from. The gospel transcends racial barriers and what we find foreshadowed in the gracious attitude of Boaz, as he from Bethlehem reaches out to Ruth from Moab, is simply an indication of how the gospel is going to stretch throughout the whole world.

- *Consider the make-up of your church membership. What barriers do you need to cross so that the gospel message reaches those in your community?*
- *What are the barriers within your church that need to be crossed if you are to be a united body of Christ, showing grace and favour to each other?*

Ruth was discovering this kindness on the path of duty. She continues to work away and as she works away, we find that her commitment is not lessened in any way. There's no hint of her attempting to leave early on the strength of the boss's interest in her. If the boss likes you, maybe you should add an extra fifteen minutes to your day to repay his kindness to you.

What a wonderful picture as she heads home. As she gets up to glean, Boaz told the men 'Just look after her. Don't make her embarrassed. In fact, pull a few bits and pieces out so that it's going to make it easier for her.' Verse 17, 'Ruth then gleaned in the field until evening. Then she threshed the barley that she had gathered' and she had a disproportionate bundle. She 'carried it back to town, and her mother-in-law saw how much she had gathered.'

I wish that I could have been there to see Naomi's eyes when Ruth came along the road. She'd sent her off in the morning, she had this idea she would go and glean in the fields. She comes back and she can barely stand up with all the grain she's carrying. Then it's just as you would imagine; all these questions. Where did you glean? Where did you work? Eventually Ruth got her all calmed down and said, 'I'll tell you everything.'

Then Ruth told her mother-in-law about the one at whose place she had been working; 'And the name of the man I worked with today is Boaz' she said. 'Oh', says Naomi, 'The Lord bless him. He hasn't stopped showing kindness to the living and the dead. This man is our close relative. He is one of our kinsman redeemers.'

Then Ruth, verse 21 says, 'He even said "Stay with my workers until they finish harvesting all my grain."' It's two people interwoven with one another, committed to one another, saying 'Isn't this fantastic, think about this' and then Naomi, with maternal instincts, verse 22, said to Ruth, her daughter-in-law, 'It will be good for you, my daughter, to go with his girls, because in someone else's field you might be harmed.'

Ruth said, 'I'll do what I want, Naomi. I don't need you.' No. In verse 23 we read, 'So Ruth stayed close to the servant girls of Boaz.' She did what her mother-in-law said and she gleaned until the barley and wheat harvests finished.

Look at how it finishes, 'And she lived with her mother-in-law.' An interesting closing sentence. It's a great finish. Yes, but everybody knows she lived with her mother-in-law, that's how she was in the same house in the morning. That's not a great sentence – can't you come up with something better than that? No, because you stand back from that sentence and say, 'How good that they loved each other. How good that they lived together in peace. How good that they discover together the provision of God. How wonderful that when their lives were so marked by poverty, they should be introduced to plenty. How fantastic that Naomi, Miss Pleasant, who had been on such a bitter path, is being warmed up again by the sunshine of God's love.'

- *Ruth didn't just live with her mother-in-law, they shared each other's lives and together they saw God working in their situation. Who do you have who not only shares your life but shares your spiritual journey? Who celebrates God's grace with you and prays with you in life's struggles? How can you strengthen the spiritual element of this relationship? If you haven't already got a 'Ruth' in your life, what can you do?*

FURTHER STUDY

Just as the term 'famine' has significant implications in the Bible, so does the term 'harvest'. Look up these various references to 'harvest': Matthew 9:35-38, 1 Corinthians 9:7-12; 15:20-24, 2 Corinthians 9:6-11, Hebrews 12:11, and Revelation 14:14-20. In what different ways do the Bible writers use the term? What particular reference to the harvest challenges you most? Explain why.

REFLECTION AND RESPONSE

In silence, reflect on the particular ways God has shown his grace and favour to you this week.

As a group, pray short prayers thanking God for the many ways he has demonstrated his grace and favour to humanity, to us as Christians and us as a church body – be specific!

In twos, discuss and then pray together about how you could show grace and favour to others in the coming week. What are the situations at work that need a touch of God's grace? How could you demonstrate grace in your home? Which of your close relationships could benefit from some grace? Consider what grace would look like in each of these scenarios and how you could show it.

REVIEW OF RUTH 2:1-23

Reread Ruth 2:1-23. The story of Ruth reminds us that God is no man's debtor. In her life and in our own experience, we can see God's providence, his grace and his favour. As Boaz looked after Ruth, God provides for us and notices all the good that we do. We don't need to be anxious about the struggles in our life. We can be wholehearted in our dedication to him and we can trust him with those who are most precious to us because his wings of refuge surround us. Like Ruth our prayer can simply be, 'May I continue to find favour in your eyes, my lord. You have given me comfort and have spoken kindly to your servant' (Ruth 2:13).

POINTS TO PONDER

- What have you learnt about God?
- What have you learnt about yourself?
- What actions or attitudes do you need to change as a result?

CHAPTER 7

An audacious plan

Aim: To develop God-honouring relationships

FOCUS ON THE THEME

Naomi comes up with an audacious plan for Ruth to take the initiative and encourage Boaz to fulfil his responsibilities as the kinsman-redeemer. As she describes the plan, we get a sense of the dynamics between the two women and their love for each other. Their relationship is far removed from the stereotypical image we have of relations with the 'in-laws.' What makes a good relationship between an adult-child and their parents/in-laws? Brainstorm all the character qualities and behaviour traits needed on both sides. Use your own experience, if it has been a positive one, of how your relationship has been or discuss helpful examples you have seen in the lives of others.

Read: Ruth 3:1-5

In chapter 3 we are getting to some kind of resolution in the story. But before we get there can I first say a word concerning how we approach the Bible? There are important questions that we need to ask and they are not routinely the questions that are asked in home Bible studies. In some home Bible studies that I've found, people read a passage of Scripture and then the leader says, 'Why don't you just take a moment quietly and then I'm going to ask how this passage makes you feel?', or 'What does this passage remind you of that you would like to share?', or, worse still, 'If you had been there what would you have written?', or worst of all, 'Is there is anything in this passage that you would like to change?' Those questions are a recipe for complete and total disaster in the study of the Bible. Unfortunately they are not uncommon questions.

The questions we need to be asking are: Number 1, 'What is the passage actually saying?' Not, 'What would I like it to say?' or 'What emphasis can I place upon it?' but 'What is it saying?' Then ask the question, 'Why is it here?' – what is the context? Then ask the question; 'Why is it saying what it's saying in the way that it's saying it?' because the Bible addresses the same topic in different places from different perspectives. Finally, I think it's helpful to ask what is surprising about this passage, so that we come to the study of the Bible with a genuine sense of agnosticism, rather than saying to ourselves, 'I've heard this so many times and I know everything about this.' The more we study the Bible, the more we are aware of the fact that there is so much that we can still learn.

- *What would you say to someone who said 'Ruth is a love story, it is not meant to be analysed and picked apart as if it were an A-level text'?*

The focus in chapter 3 starts where it ended in chapter 2, with Naomi. 'One day Naomi her mother-in-law said to her, "My daughter, should I not try to find a home for you"'? It's a very interesting juxtaposition, when you think of how quickly we've moved from the very sorry circumstances of the first chapter, when Naomi urges her daughters-in-law to return home. In that situation, she saw the bottle as being half empty. Now she is reviewing the situation. The sunshine has poked through and she is beginning, at least, to see the possibility that the bottle is half full.

Chapter 2 began with the initiative of Ruth going out to gainful employment and here, in chapter 3, it begins with Naomi, who is establishing a plan of action. The story begins to pick up in pace and gives the reader the sense that we are moving towards a point of resolution. Not only has there been a change from a minor key to a major key, but the dominant theme is establishing itself.

- *Scan through chapter 2. Review all that has happened in the story so far that would make Naomi feel hopeful again.*

We begin to pick up this dominant theme as we notice in verses 1, 2, 3, 4 and 5 that Naomi has come up with what we can only refer to as an audacious plan.

There are certain situations which, when we first encounter them, may seem peculiar to us but when, after a bit of reflection, we peruse the circumstances again, we say, 'That really is fairly straightforward.' But this plan is not such an instance. No matter how often you read what Naomi suggests here, you will not fail to be forcibly struck by the sheer bravado that is necessary if this plan is going to be implemented. I wish I could have been there, just a fly on the wall, to watch the eyes of Ruth widen as Naomi approaches her in this way.

She suggests something that no mother is going to suggest as a plan of action to her daughter going off to live in a dorm at University; at least, no sensible mother. In fact, what she suggests is akin to the kind of experiment that is shown from time to time on television and across the bottom of the screen a message is continually scrolling saying 'Do not attempt this at home.' Because what we have here needs to be understood within a context that is actually quite different in every dimension from all that we know about marriage and courtship and interpersonal relationships between the sexes. That's why I suggested to you that these points of interpretive approach are of vital necessity because we could do ourselves a great disservice by launching from twelfth century BC Palestine into twenty-first century Bradford. We could make a dreadful mess. There are dimensions to this, historically, culturally and socially, that we can only begin to get an inkling of but we cannot speak forcibly about.

We have an indication of how Naomi is thinking. We can almost see her mind ticking over. She looks at Ruth and says, 'Boaz is such a nice man. Boaz is a relative. Boaz has been kind to you. Don't you think I should try and find a home for you? Tonight, he'll be winnowing barley on the threshing floor, therefore get yourself cleaned up, washed up, perfumed up, dressed up and go down to the threshing floor.' Do you believe in arranged marriages, that's the question?

I think everybody believes in arranged marriages. We all believe in arranged marriages; the only question is who's arranging the marriages. I have the privilege of speaking to the students who are teaching the children at the Keswick Convention. Yesterday I spoke very straightforwardly to these young people about the importance of paying attention to those who love them most when they are making decisions about their life's partner.

Now an ancient commentator redresses the balance. He says:

> Parents in giving advice, ought to have solely in view the happiness of their children when advising re marriage. They ought not to choose for sons and daughters those most

agreeable to themselves, i.e. to the parents but all things considered those most likely to make their children glad. Gentle persuasions and serious advice may frequently be of good use. Compulsion belongs not to a parent but to a tyrant.

I think that's very helpful. Just a point to make in passing, think how many young people are in dreadful straits because they wouldn't listen to those who loved them best and cared for them most.

- *If you are a parent, to what extent have you been able to speak to your child about relationships? What circumstances or situations have been most conducive to broaching the subject?*
- *What influence should parents have on their children's marriages? What should their role be and how should it change before and after the marriage ceremony?*
- *Family relationships and courtship can be very complicated. What advice would you give the individuals in the following scenarios?*
  - *A young woman became a Christian at university and wants to marry someone she met at the Christian Union. Her parents, who are not Christians, are unhappy with her choice, fearing she will soon pass through this religious phase and find herself in an awkward relationship. What should the woman do? To what extent should she listen to her parents and seek to placate them? What would be a wise way to handle this situation?*
  - *A young Christian couple have been dating for sometime. Their families on both sides are Christians and are very supportive of the match. Friends and church folk have spoken about how well suited they are and a wedding announcement is expected soon. Everyone seems to think*

a marriage would be in God's will but the young man is having doubts. He feels swept along by the tide of opinion and asks you what he should do.
- *A Christian woman is in a serious relationship with a non-Christian. Her parents don't know whether to speak to her about their concerns, in case they become estranged from their daughter. If marriage is in view they want to keep on friendly terms with the young man.*

- *Consider the people in your church whose parents are not Christians. What kind of support do they need? How can individuals and the church provide this support for them?*
- *In an arranged marriage the twenty-first century romantic view of love is not a priority. How does the Bible view love in the context of marriage? See Ephesians 5:22-33.*

This is a strange venture though; a risky and daring venture. Naomi has conceived it, she is presumably trusting God and she's believing in the character of Boaz, such as she knows it, and she is suggesting to Ruth to take this course of action. Boaz is a man of standing, true, but we might add he is also still just a man and the best of men are men at best. There is no question that this is a vulnerable, tricky strategy and we could spend a long time reflecting on it and whether we think it's a good idea or not.

Having said all of that, while we may not be as ingenious as Naomi, we shouldn't overlook the privilege and responsibility, not only of helping our own youngsters, if we have them, but also of helping others who are under our care. In America at the moment and, I presume, across here too because of the nature of the internet, there is a website called Eharmony.com. I'm not recommending it, I'm just identifying it. It's a dating service on the internet and it is adding names at a rate of ten thousand people a day. People are signing on, asking for help in profiling themselves; socially, economically, psychologically and so on, in order that they might then be listed on this site and might find someone compatible with them with whom they may spend the rest of their lives.

That represents a crying need in the culture, presumably. If ten thousand a day are prepared to go into cyber-space to meet a potential marriage partner, we are not going to condemn Naomi for doing what she did. This was a good move on Naomi's part. Can I suggest, in passing, that those of us who are married and who have homes should be endeavouring always to put single people together and to do so with an eye for detail and an awareness of who they are? A lot of single people don't like the idea but they are desperately longing to meet someone with whom they may spend their time, unless they've been given a gift of singleness. Many of us have occasion to be thankful for those friends who saw us and another person and created a context in which, around a meal table, in the company of many people, we could meet.

If you're going to do this, you have to be very careful and that's what Naomi is as well. 'Wait until he's finished his meal. Note where he sleeps, I mean, you don't want to wake up in the middle of the night lying next to the wrong person's feet. And uncover his feet and lie down.' Now in the uncovering of his feet there is clearly a sign that is being sent to Boaz which is more than simply 'Who stole my blanket?' The uncovering of feet was symbolic. It was a gesture which would be meaningful and, as we discover in the story, it turned out to be so.

- *How could the church cater better for singles? Consider how the church relates to those who are divorced, those who are widowed, single parents and those who have never married.*

The opening scene of this audacious plan concludes in verse 5 with this great expression of devotion on the part of Ruth: 'I will do whatever you say.' She had shown her devotion to Naomi in chapter 1 by not doing what she said: Naomi said 'Go home' and Ruth said, 'I'm not going to go home, I'm devoted to you.' Here in chapter 3 she shows her devotion to Naomi by doing exactly what she said.

- *The relationship between Christ and the church is described in the Bible as a marriage. Readers of the Old Testament would understand this to be an arranged marriage. What new insight does this give you into the type of relationship Christ has with the church? How does the arranged marriage between Ruth and Boaz demonstrate the dynamics of our relationship with Christ?*

FURTHER STUDY

As you read your Bible this week, study it as suggested above. Choose a passage, read it a few times and then ask the following questions:

- What is the passage actually saying?
- Why is it here? – i.e. what is the context?
- Why is it saying what it's saying in the way that it's saying it?
- What is surprising about this passage?

It may help to write down the answers to these questions. When you have established what God wanted to communicate in these verses, consider how his message applies to you. Is there a challenge or an encouragement you need to take on board? An attitude you need to change? A promise you need to believe? Take time to consider what God is saying to you and how you need to respond.

REFLECTION AND RESPONSE

Spend time reflecting on the issues that this passage has raised:

- Are you disappointed when you consider your own family relationships?

- Do you recognise that you haven't listened to the concern and wisdom of those who love you?
- Is there some action you can take to improve your family relationships?
- Is there some action you can take to improve your relationship with certain individuals in the church?
- Are there groups within the church community that God is challenging you to help – the widows, singles, those without Christian parents or those with difficult family backgrounds, for example?

Consider what God wants you to do or what attitudes he wants you to change as a result of this study and then respond like Ruth, 'I will do whatever you say.'

If it is appropriate, you could share these thoughts with the group and pray together about them.

CHAPTER 8

Cold feet and redemption

Aim: To develop a more Christ-like character

FOCUS ON THE THEME

This chapter highlights the Christ-like characters of Ruth and Boaz. As Naomi's audacious plan unfolds, we recognise Ruth's resourcefulness, humility and obedience and Boaz's integrity, honour and graciousness.

What character traits impress and appeal to you most? Imagine you were meeting a group of people for the first time, what type of person would you be drawn to and why? Share your thoughts with the group.

Read: Ruth 3:6-18

Verse 6 takes us down onto the threshing floor but before we get there, we just need to fill in a little bit of background. Before Naomi's plan is executed, it is imperative that we understand at least enough of the instruction of the Law of Moses to grasp this unfolding drama. The Law of Moses made provision for those who had become destitute as a result of the death of a spouse. When a man died, leaving no children, provision was made. When property had been sold in order to ease the poverty situation, God's law stipulated that a kinsman redeemer would make the purchase necessary to secure the property for the impoverished family. This also ensured that the land of Israel would remain within the families of Israel. In the same way, the brother or another close relative within the structure of the family would marry the widow in order to produce a child, so as to continue the family name in Israel. This is referred to as Levirate marriage. It comes from *levir*, which is the Latin word translating the Hebrew for 'brother-in-law', as it was the place of the brother-in-law or a close relative to take on this responsibility.

These provisions in relationship to property and to an heir matched the circumstances we have here in the lives of Naomi and Ruth. Since Boaz was one of their kinsman redeemers, as he has been identified back in chapter 2, it seemed wise to approach him. Naomi, with that understanding, then conceives of this strategy which she asks Ruth to implement.

The strategic plan in verses 1-5 is executed between verses 6-13 in the midnight hour. Look at Ruth. 'I will do anything you say' she answered and she went down to the threshing floor. It's clear this is not a fool's errand; she understands exactly what this is about. Ruth is a wonderful person. I don't know what Boaz looked like. He may have had hair growing out of everywhere, you didn't know which side you were looking at when you saw him. And there's every reason to believe that she had her whole future in front of her and then her mother-in-law says, 'What about Boaz? He's a nice man, a relative and you need a home.' Ruth isn't saying 'This is all about me.' She is still thinking about Naomi. 'If this would be helpful then I'm prepared to have a stab at it.'

Down to the threshing floor she goes and she did everything her mother-in-law told her to do. 'When Boaz had finished eating and drinking and was in good spirits, he went over to lie down at the far end of the grain pile.' Don't let's romanticise this. I don't agree with the commentators who make out this is a very sexual, sensual experience. The fellow was lying down next to the equivalent of a huge pile of Brussel sprouts. This is not some hotel in the inner city and she's sneaking up to his room. He's lying down by a big bag of barley, snoring presumably. This is not an attractive proposition! It is obedience that takes her there.

- *Why is Ruth's obedience to Naomi's request so impressive? What were the dangers and risks associated with the plan?*

Having uncovered his feet, she lies down. Notably, it doesn't say she slept but she lay down. And in the middle of the night he wakes with a start. Maybe it's his response to the cold. You can imagine him, all of a sudden, waking up and thinking to himself, 'My feet are freezing' and then looking down at his feet and saying 'Who took the blanket?' He reaches for the blanket and tugs on it, it's not coming and he looks down and says 'What's that?' and then 'Who's that?' She says, 'I am your servant, Ruth. Spread the corner of your garment over me since you are a kinsman redeemer.'

The man of standing is lying on the floor, next to a strange woman. What is he going to do next? How is he going to react? Is he going to be angry? Is he going to say, 'Get out of here! What's this about?' Is he going to stay in befuddled confusion and make no response at all or grab his blanket back and go to sleep saying, 'I don't know what that's about but I'm not paying attention to it tonight, I'll deal with it in the morning. My feet are freezing.' Whether he realises it or not, this is his cue. Go back to verse 4: Naomi has it all set out. 'When he lies down, note the place where he is lying. Then go and uncover his feet and lie down. He will tell you what to do.'

- *Boaz found himself in a potentially embarrassing situation. A vulnerable young woman, lying at his feet, not only put his honour to the test but was open to misinterpretation by others. What steps can we take to preserve the integrity of our character? Think about:*
  - *Practical measures you could take to avoid temptation.*
  - *Spiritual disciplines you could practice to give you strength to resist temptation.*
- *Boaz had to respond quickly to the urgency of the situation. What have crisis situations revealed about your character? What have they revealed about your trust in God?*

But Ruth goes off script. She decides she's going to ask him to do something before he gets the chance to tell her what to do. 'Why don't you spread the corner of your garment over me?' She invites him, in this strange gesture, to assume a willingness for all the privileges and responsibilities of marriage.

It is true that out of the abundance of the heart a man speaks. Out of the abundance of Boaz's heart he then speaks. Notice how quickly the name of the Lord is on his lips, 'The LORD bless you.' Incidentally, in interpersonal relationships with those of the opposite sex, it is always good to keep the name of the Lord on our lips and close to our lips, that Jesus, Lord and King, may be introduced at any point in any situation.

- *If someone heard a recording of your conversation at home, would they think you were a Christian? What does your speech say about you and how can you improve it?*
- *How easy do you find it to talk about the Lord? Consider how freely you would initiate a conversation about God in the following scenarios:*
  - *When you're spending an evening alone with your husband/wife.*

  - *When you have invited a couple from church to your home for a meal.*
  - *When you have a tradesman working in your home for the week.*
  - *When you're talking with your neighbour.*
  - *When you're chatting to a shop assistant as you pay for your goods.*
- *When you bring God into the conversation you are having with your spouse or close friends, what difference does it make to what you say, how you respond, and the flow of the discussion?*

He introduces the Lord to the conversation. He expresses his kindness for this young lady. 'My daughter', he says, a wonderful tenderness that acknowledges the significance of their age difference. He then commends her, 'You've outdone yourself. This is an amazing kindness. You left your homeland and your family out of devotion to Naomi. That was an expression of your love. But now you're taking it to another level. This is amazing. You haven't run after the younger men, whether rich or poor.' In other words, he says, 'You could have married for love or you could have married for money but the fact that you are here in the middle of the night, making this proposal on the strength of family loyalty, is an expression of *hesed* love.' In the New Testament, it is *agape* love.

- *To what extent should family loyalty be a character trait of a Christian? What priority should we give to family loyalty? The following references may be helpful – Matthew 19:29, Luke 14:26, Ephesians 6:2-3, 1 Timothy 5:4, 8.*

Can I say a word about equality of age in marriage? Because there is such a disparity here and people get themselves dreadfully worked up about what age everybody is and whether you can only propose if you're a woman in a leap year. I think some girls ought to propose because if it's at all here as it is in America, we've got a lot of men in their thirties that are totally inept and walking around in a dream. They don't have the foggiest idea how to get from A to B. If you took a dozen of them and laid them end to end, they couldn't reach a conclusion and what is necessary is the initiative of the women.

But just a word in relationship to the disparity of age. Age disparity matters about as much as physical beauty matters. It matters about as much as financial security matters or natural charm matters and none of those matter very much at all in the end. None of them, or all of them together can take the place of virtue, integrity and selflessness.

What does Boaz identify in Ruth? Her noble character. What is it that has marked this woman out upon her return? Boaz doesn't say, 'All the guys on the harvest team say that you're the best looking girl that has been in Bethlehem for years.' He says, 'No, the word on the street is that you are a noble character and it is your character that is so commendable to me.' So his answer is 'Yes.' He says 'I'll be glad to do that. However, there is a fly in the ointment. We have one little problem. Because, although I am a kinsman redeemer, there is another kinsman redeemer nearer than me.'

- *Again and again we are struck by the importance of character in this story. How can we learn about character? What programmes, places, people and practices should we associate with if we want to develop a more Christ-like character?*

What a great story. The pace slows up. When we are expecting resolution to the story, into the drama comes the possibility that everything that the audience is hoping for, finally the great acclaim when Boaz and Ruth are married, might not happen. The audience, having breathed a great sigh of relief, is now anxiously saying 'Is Boaz going to lose Ruth after all this? What are you doing, Boaz? She likes you. Who else would take you on? Why do you have to mention this other chap? Look, she's at your feet in the middle of the night, perfumed up and proposing and you get into some legal technicality.'

Boaz was a man of standing. Ruth wouldn't have wanted to marry somebody who went round the edges. No girl wants to marry someone who's in sales and is a liar and tells the people that he's selling to that he's able to supply the windows a week from Friday, although he knows that they're on back order and will not be available for another two months. If you are going out with a boy who does that, then get away from him until he gets himself sorted out and, if he never does, then get away from him for good because the boy you want to commit your life to, the girl you want to commit your life to, is a girl, is a boy who consistently asks, question number 1 in any decision, 'What is the right thing to do?' Boaz says, 'I must do the right thing, therefore I have to tell you that this may not end up the way that you envisage but the right thing must be done.'

- *How should we respond, what should our character be like, if we realize too late that we've married someone whose character we don't admire?*

He says, 'You'd better stay here tonight. When you leave, go quietly.' It wouldn't be good for her to be seen leaving, although everything had been above board. Her actions would have been open to misinterpretation and if there had been any hint of moral impropriety, it would have an immediate impact on the legal proceedings that were about to take place the following morning.

'So she lay at his feet until morning', verse 14, and she got up before she could be recognised, in those murky hours of the morning. 'He also said, "Bring me the shawl you're wearing and hold it out."' She probably had one of these big things that went over her head and when she did so, he poured into it six measures of barley and put it on her and then he went back to town.

This is the hardest part in the whole of these chapters for me. I don't understand why Boaz gave Ruth the barley. But the commentator Hubbard, whose sandals I am unworthy to unloose, suggests that, since Ruth's return is potentially embarrassing, it required precautions and the six measures of barley are used as a cover-up. So, let's say you suggest to somebody, 'I want you to slip home quietly but here, put on your head seven stone of barley so that no one notices you.' Unless everybody's walking up the street with seven stone of barley on their head, you're going to look conspicuous. I'm befuddled by this. The best way I can explain it is that if somebody saw Ruth walking home with nothing on her head they would be suspicious, but if they saw her with the seven stone of barley on her head, they would assume she was working the night shift and was just getting home in the morning.

The breakfast report begins in verse 16. 'When Ruth came to her mother-in-law, Naomi asked, "How did it go, my daughter?"' Then she told her everything Boaz had done for her and added 'He gave me these six measures of barley'. Lawson characteristically makes this lovely comment. He takes this phrase, 'Then she told her everything' and says, 'Let no young woman deal in secrecy and concealment. Let her beware of doing anything that she would not want her affectionate mother to know.' Ask two questions before you do anything. 'Would I do this if this was the last five minutes of my life?' And, two, 'Am I able to do this and then make a full disclosure to my mother when I next look into her eyes?'

The barley is worthy of more careful attention than I am apparently giving to it because this statement, 'Don't go back to your mother-in-law empty-handed' or 'empty' should ring bells for the reader. Remember that was Naomi's great statement indicative of her bitter condition in 1:21, 'I went out full and the LORD hath brought me home again empty' (King James Version). Boaz says to Ruth, 'I want you to go back bearing all of this barley. I don't want you to go back to your mother-in-law empty.'

There were two kinds of emptiness represented in the life of Naomi; the emptiness of childlessness and the emptiness of her tummy as a result of famine and, with the provision of this grain in amazing abundance, Boaz is saying through Ruth to Naomi, 'You can forget worrying about what you are going to eat ever again. That is all taken care of. All of that emptiness is dealt with.' The Hebrew in verse 21 of chapter 1 where Naomi says 'Full I went out and empty I return' can connote childlessness. If it can connote childlessness in chapter 1 then it may connote the same thing here. The grain is a suitable symbol of offspring to come. Hubbard: 'the seed to fill the stomach was promise of the seed to fill the womb.' Begg: 'Ruth has arrived home with a bundle for she and Naomi to enjoy and the prospect of the arrival of another little bundle is likely in the near future.'

This big bundle represents God's answer to the dilemma to which Naomi could see no answer when she left Moab. 'Go back Orpah, go back Ruth. There is no future, there is no possibility. Here I am the empty one. There is no chance that my emptiness may be met.' As she takes the breakfast report from her daughter-in-law she realises that God is able to do exceedingly abundantly beyond all that she can ask or even imagine.

Naomi has the last word. 'Wait, my daughter, until you find out what happens. I don't think that Boaz is going to let the grass grow under his feet.'

A couple of words in conclusion. Naomi's ingenious plan has been carried out to perfection by Ruth. What Naomi had prayed would be part and parcel of Ruth and Orpah's lives is about to be answered in a far more wonderful way than she could have ever conceived. In the freedom of the actions of these individuals, God's providence has been at work using even wrong choices and strange ones to conform everything to the eternal counsel of his will. As we await the final instalment of the story, we see how Boaz points forward to the Lord Jesus. For Jesus Christ is our kinsman redeemer, becoming like us, identifying with us in every way and yet without sin. And when we, like Ruth, cast ourselves at the feet of Jesus, depending on his mercy, aware of the fact that we are outsiders, he grants forgiveness, he welcomes us with a steadfast love and he loads us down with his benefits. In the Lord Jesus we are granted one benefit after another. Boaz takes Ruth to himself, sharing his life and abundance with her. By redeeming us Jesus makes us his bride, we have a Saviour to whom we may go and we have a Saviour for whom we may live.

- *Think back over the last year. How has your character developed as you've seen God work in your life? What particular character trait, with God's help, do you want to work on in the next twelve months?*

FURTHER STUDY

'Fullness' is an important term in the book of Ruth. The Apostle Paul also uses the term frequently in the New Testament. Look at Ephesians 1:23, 3:19, 4:13 and Colossians 1:19, 25, 2:9, 10. What ideas is Paul trying to convey here? What in particular strikes you from these Bible verses?

REFLECTION AND RESPONSE

This story reminds us of the value of character and how it impacts all that we do and all that we are. Two different aspects of character are summed up in this idea of 'having a standing.' Boaz is described as a 'man of standing' (2:1) because of his integrity and honour. Ruth, in her humility, recognises she has no standing – no reason to boast or to be shown grace (2:13).

As a group, pray for each other that you would be men and women of 'standing' in the workplace, home and community. Pray for those in the group and wider church who are involved in business and have community links. Pray that God would help preserve their integrity, protect their testimony from disrepute and give wisdom for the decisions that need to be made.

Pray too that, like Ruth, we'd remember we have no standing before God – we have no reason to boast, no achievements or credentials which will impress him. All that we are and have is from him. Praise God that he has shown his love to us and even treated us like his sons. Use verses such as Isaiah 61;10, Psalm 103:1-15 and Romans 5:8 to meditate on as you sing, pray and praise God together.

REVIEW OF RUTH 3:1-18

Reread Ruth 3:1-18. Naomi's plan for Ruth to marry Boaz is set in motion and is a perfect backdrop to display godly characters and relationships. Earlier Boaz recognised that Ruth had taken refuge under God's wings of protection (2:12) and now he realises that he was to be the means of that protection as she lay down under the 'wings' of his garment (3:7). He was also the means by which Naomi's emptiness would become fullness again. As the kinsman-redeemer he came into these women's lives and totally transformed them. Jesus is our kinsman-redeemer – he shares our humanity but he is also our Saviour whose death on the cross brings us forgiveness and a future to look forward to. Like Boaz, Jesus transforms our lives and brings us into his family.

POINTS TO PONDER

- What have you learnt about God?
- What have you learnt about yourself?
- What actions or attitudes do you need to change as a result?

CHAPTER 9

An old sandal and a new wife

Aim: To consider God's view of marriage

FOCUS ON THE THEME

In this chapter Boaz marries Ruth. We see his commitment to her and the involvement of the whole community as they pray and witness the event. God designed marriage for our benefit but his ideas for how marriage should work seem to have been ignored by contemporary society.

How does our society view marriage? Look at newspaper and magazine articles to find out what people think about marriage, what elements of marriage are important to them, and how they view the marriage commitment. If you have people of different ages in the group, you could talk together about how society's view of marriage has changed over the years – the good and bad points.

Read: Ruth 4:1-13

At the end of chapter 3, Naomi has issued the instruction to Ruth to 'Wait, my daughter, until you find out what happens.' Waiting is often very difficult for us and both

Naomi and Ruth are like the readers, sitting on the edge of their seats. The resolution of the story apparently hinges on the response of an unknown character who is about to be posed this most important question.

Chapter 4 begins 'Meanwhile, Boaz went up to the town gate and sat there.' There is a lot of sitting around at the end of chapter 3 and here at the beginning of chapter 4. He's sitting with purpose in the public square, in the place where business was transacted and legal matters were settled. People moving in the early morning to their places of work and to places of opportunity would perhaps have spoken to him on the way. Clearly, Boaz knew that it was a big day. It was a big day for him and for Ruth but he could never have known the part he was playing in the scheme of redemptive history.

Why is Boaz sitting in the public square at all? The reason he put himself in this position is because he is committed to doing the right thing. As a man of standing he operates on the basis of principle. He is not prepared to take the easy route. He is not making decisions on the basis of consensus but on the basis of conviction. He has made it clear to Ruth that if they are to be brought together it will be down the line of duty, of moral rectitude. It is vitally important always to ask what is the right thing to do and not least of all when the thing that we are considering doing is marriage.

Boaz is sitting in the public square so that he can resolve this matter with the nearer kinsman redeemer. He puts himself in a position to meet this man if he happens to come along. And the initiative of Boaz is rewarded. It's interesting that when you take initiative how often this happens; when you step out in a spirit of prayerful dependence upon God.

He calls to the character, 'Come over here, my friend, and sit down.' We said in the opening study that the author is clearly interested in the names that are given to us in the book. If that is an accurate observation then it must surely be significant that the author chooses not to give us the name of this particular person. Because this fellow is never named, he's a complete no-name and the commentators can get three or four or five pages out of the significance of the fact that he has no name. They conclude that either the writer cares about him and wants to save him embarrassment for posterity's sake or he is exercising a measure of judgement on this individual by refusing to name him, since this chap is so concerned to preserve his family name. It's a wonderful paradox. The one who is so concerned about securing the rights to his family name is not remembered and the one who is selflessly concerned for the needs of others is, of course, remembered for his kindness. We are not to miss that little principle.

Remember when they approached John the Baptist and they said 'John, what do you have to say about yourself?' That's the kind of question many of us like to hear. The answer to that is, 'Why don't you sit down and let me tell you about myself.' But that's not the response of John the Baptist. He says, 'I'm a finger pointing, I'm a light shining, I'm a voice shouting, "Prepare ye the way of the Lord." My name is unimportant, his name is the important name. He is the one who has been given a name that is above every name, that at the name of Jesus, every knee should bow.' Mr. Concerned-about-his-name isn't given a name and Mr. Not-concerned-about-himself is remembered for ever. Let each of us beware of trying to make a name for ourselves.

Once Boaz has got the fellow in position, he calls ten of the elders. The way in which he is able to implement his strategy so straightforwardly and quickly suggests that his standing in the community is significant. 'Excuse me sir, would you please sit down.' He sits down. Then he takes ten of the elders and he says to them, 'Sit here.' 'So you sit there, I'll sit here and you sit there' and, look, verse 2 'and they did so.' Boaz is not a bossy character; he is just someone who has influence. With great skill, he presents the issue.

First there's the property to discuss: 'You're a kinsman-redeemer, a piece of land is for sale, it belonged to our brother Elimelech. I thought I should bring the matter to your attention and suggest that you buy it in the presence of those seated here and in the presence of the elders of my people. However, if you choose not to, I am next in line.' Everybody's watching in the wings, seeing the drama unfold, holding their breath to see what he will say and, 'Oh no', he says, 'I will redeem it.' There is a big intake of breath on the part of the audience. They said, 'Oh, no, this isn't how it's supposed to go. He can't redeem it. What's happening to the story?'

Then Boaz says to him, 'Now before you start taking your sandals off, you ought to know that, along with the land, you get a wife.' The provision of the law, as we have seen, in respect to property and posterity was all about the preservation of the family and the property that was still held by Naomi went in equity and in law with the hand of Ruth. So, suddenly, the circumstances are different from those initially presented and this gentleman has to wrestle with the implications of not only becoming the owner of another piece of property but also becoming the husband of another wife.

Becoming the husband of a wife is something that ought to be taken very carefully and seriously. As the information is presented to this character, he has to wrestle with the implications. Privilege, opportunity, duty and responsibility go hand in hand and, to his credit, the man answers with great honesty. Verse 6, 'At this, the kinsman redeemer said, "Then I cannot redeem it"' and he explains why. If he was only required to buy the land then, although he would pay the purchase price, he would still have an accruing asset but if he were to take on a wife with the land, and they were then to have children. Then the child would be the heir to the land that he had purchased. Therefore it would be no ultimate economic benefit to him and there was the distinct possibility with the unfolding and interweaving of life that that child or the heirs of this marriage might then become part of the ultimate disbursement of his resources and he didn't want to jeopardise his retirement strategy. So he said in verse 6, 'I cannot redeem it because I might endanger my own estate. You redeem it yourself. I cannot do it.'

- *What are the privileges and opportunities of marriage?*
- *What are the duties and responsibilities for a husband and a wife within marriage?*

This brings us to the sandal swap which was used to finalise the redemption and transfer of property in the early days of Israel's history. This was the method of legalising transactions in Israel. As the details of the transaction are formalised, the crowd is cheering in the grandstand. But they are not simply cheering; it's really a praying crowd. The book, incidentally, is full of prayer, on the lips of all these different characters: 'May the LORD show kindness to you', 'May the LORD be with you', 'May the LORD repay you', 'May the LORD bless you', 'May the LORD grant your favour' and so on.

This response is expressed clearly in the prayer of the elders for Ruth in verse 11. 'Then the elders and all those at the gate said "We are witnesses, and let's just have a word of prayer for Ruth. And our prayer for Ruth is this, 'May the LORD make the woman who is coming into your home like Rachel and Leah who together built up the house of Israel.'"' Rachel and Leah were the founding mothers of Israel. 'And may we also have a word of prayer for Boaz. Our prayer for Boaz is this, "May you have standing in Ephrathah and be famous in Bethlehem."'

And there's also a prayer for the family, verse 12. 'Through the offspring the LORD gives you by this young woman, may your family be like that of Perez.' Perez, who was also born of a foreigner, became a famous clan chief in the nation.

- *Look at the prayers the elders say for Ruth, Boaz and their family in chapter 4:11-12. How do you feel about their prayer requests? Would you pray these requests for someone today? Explain your answer.*
- *What should we be praying for husbands, wives and families today? What are the greatest needs and pressures on families?*

This prayerful response on the part of the elders follows the careful way Boaz presented everything to them. His detailed concern is related largely to the eventuality of the commitment he is making. Hubbard says of his statement before the witnesses 'It is solemn, precise and strikingly detailed.' There can be no doubt that Boaz was anticipating all of the benefits that marriage would bring. But you will notice in verse 10 that his purpose is greater than that. 'I have also acquired Ruth the Moabitess, Mahlon's widow, as my wife ... so that I may live happily ever after. So that she and I may go on vacation together. So that she may rub my back when I come home.'

No. 'I have acquired Ruth the Moabitess, Mahlon's widow as my wife', notice, 'in order to maintain the name of the dead with his property.' What are you doing here, Boaz? He is amazed at the kindness that she has shown to Naomi. We should be equally amazed at the phenomenal commitment that he makes to this family. His desires are not driven by his sensual appetites. His commitment in this case is striking.

Again, if you check in the East with those whose marriages have been arranged and have learned to love one another as a result of this prior commitment, you will find that, statistically, they have stayed married far longer than those who tried to learn to love and then eventually made a commitment. That's not an argument for anything, it's simply an observation.

- *Why do more and more people struggle with the idea of commitment?*
- *How would you respond to someone who said, 'Marriage is about love, the marriage relationship should come naturally, it shouldn't be about effort and discipline'?*

Then in verse 13 the story shifts from the boardroom to the bedroom, so to speak. 'So Boaz took Ruth and she became his wife. Then he went to her and the LORD enabled her to conceive and she gave birth to a son.'

As marriages crumble, as legal institutions seek to redefine it, as Christians lose their voice to address it because of pre-marital sex, extra-marital sex and total confusion in their minds, society hastens down a road on a fast train with apparently no driver. Therefore when we come to the Bible and it expresses the concerns in the heart of God in relationship to marriage, we need to, in these days, pay very careful attention to it.

'For this reason, a man will leave his father and mother and be united to his wife and the two will become one flesh.' That is not some arbitrary thing which has been conceived in a moment of time. Marriage is not a contrivance of man. Marriage is a creation ordinance. God cares about all marriages. He has established it. He has laid it down and the order of things is vital. Leaving, cleaving, interweaving, conceiving; I leave, I cleave, I interweave, we conceive. To alter the structure is to bring chaos into our lives and into the life of society. This order, which is by God's design, cannot be tampered with without harm to all.

Notice that the story follows exactly this order of things. Boaz took Ruth, she became his wife, he went to her and the Lord gave the gift of children. Nobody was in any doubt in the community, nor should they have been, because marriage is a personal thing but it's not a private thing.

- *What is the point of marriage for those who aren't Christians? What value would obeying God in this area have for them?*
- *How should the church and individual Christians respond to other Christians who have conceived a child outside marriage? What are the various factors to consider in our response?*

Young couples today say. 'We're not going to have a very public thing, in fact we're going away to a hotel, two thousand miles away, just two or three of us and we're going to get married. I'm saving my father a lot of money.' I always say to them, 'I think you should really, really reconsider that.' 'Why?' 'Because marriage is personal but it isn't private.'

There's a reason why the leaving and cleaving is supposed to be public. That's why they posted the banns so that everybody in the community would be able to say 'Spinster from Parish X is about to be united with Bachelor in Parish Y. And if anyone knows any just cause why they may not be lawfully joined together in marriage, let him now declare it or else forever after be quiet. And I require and charge you both that if either of you know any reason why you may not be lawfully joined together that you do now declare it.'

In America the couples come and say, 'Please don't say that part, Alistair, because we don't like that. It's scary.'

And I say, 'I love it being scary. I'm going to say it and I'm going to pause for a long time at the end of the questions.' Just to make the point!

When the car drives away with the girl and her husband, the people are supposed to look out the window and say, 'When she comes back she will be different from the way in which she left.' She's supposed to go away as a virgin. She's supposed to come back from her honeymoon as having been interweaved with her husband. Do you know how seldom that takes place, even in the Christian community? Why? Because people are downright disobedient. But if Jesus is Lord, then I am not at liberty to disbelieve what the Lord Jesus teaches. Nor am I at liberty to disobey what the Lord Jesus demands of my behaviour.

Bonhoeffer said, 'Marriage is more than your love for each other. It has a higher dignity and power, for it is God's holy ordinance. In your love you see only the heaven of your happiness but in marriage you are placed at a post of responsibility towards the world and mankind.'

Your love is your own private possession but marriage is something more than personal. It is a status, it is an office that joins you together in the sight of God and man and that is why the minister says to the couple,

> It is therefore not to be entered upon lightly or carelessly but thoughtfully, with reverence to God, with due consideration of the purposes for which it was established by God. It was established for the lifelong companionship, help and strength which husband and wife ought to give to each other. It was established for the continuance of family life, that children who are gifts from the Lord should be brought up and trained to love and obey God and it was established for the welfare of human society, which can be strong and healthy only when the marriage bond is held in order.

- *What does it mean to be 'joined together in the sight of God'? Does it mean never sleeping a night away from your spouse, sharing the same opinion, or something else? What happens to your individuality when you get married?*

If the Christian church will not stand up for the nature of marriage, then no one will. The chances of withstanding the tides of this are so miniscule, it is unthinkable to anticipate the lifestyle amongst which our grandchildren and great-grandchildren will grow. So it is no strange consideration to pray 'Oh, that you would rend the heavens and come down. Oh, God, that you would come and, in judgement, first begin with the people of God' – and that we would get our own act cleaned up ourselves.'

How discreetly the Bible deals with sex. I love it. How disgustingly so many pulpiteers tackle this subject. It's embarrassing even to be in their company as they speak about it. In the Bible the place of marriage, the place of interpersonal relationships and sexual union are dealt with in decorum and discretion, making it clear that sex is within and only within the framework of a heterosexual monogamous lifelong commitment. That it is within the framework of continuity, reliability and permanence and it is within that dimension that God gives the gift of children.

- *How should the church deal with the subject of sex and relationships? How can it tackle the issue with discretion, given how much young people are exposed to it from an early age in society? How can the church persuade people to keep sex for marriage?*

- *What relevance does the book of Ruth have if you are unmarried? Consider chapter 4:1-12 in particular; what lessons are there for us, regardless of our marital status?*

FURTHER STUDY

It is interesting in the story of Ruth that all the family members are named but the nearest kinsman-redeemer remains anonymous. The paradox is that Boaz, unconcerned about his family name, is remembered forever whereas the other man, who was concerned about posterity, cannot be recalled. The Bible has an interesting perspective on names. Look at the following references – Genesis 11:1-9, 12:1-2; 1 Chronicles 17:8, 2 Chronicles 7:14; Romans 9:17; 1 Corinthians 3:3-8; Philippians 2:5-11. What do you learn about the significance of names, how one's name becomes truly great and the greatness of God's name? If you have a concordance, you could look up other Bible verses for a wider search.

REFLECTION AND RESPONSE

In silence, reflect upon the issues arising from this week's study. You could pray:

- For your spouse.
- About problems in your marriage.
- For your children, that they would keep sex for marriage.

As a group, copy the example of the elders and pray for wives, husbands and families. Go back to the answers you wrote on the flip chart about the needs and pressures for families and spend time praying through this list. Encourage each member of the group to pray for another group member's family regularly.

CHAPTER 10

The mystery of history

Aim: To see our lives in the context of God's salvation plan

FOCUS ON THE THEME

In these last few verses of the book of Ruth, the author steps back and gives us a panoramic view of God's work in history and where these two women fit into his salvation plan.

Ruth and Naomi probably never knew that king David, and ultimately Jesus, would descend from their family line. Likewise, most of the time we don't know how God is using us in redemption history. Sometimes, however, he give us a glimpse. If God has used you in some way to help another person become a Christian, share with the group what happened – you may have just had a brief conversation with the person, perhaps you had the opportunity to share the gospel, or you may have simply given them a tract and heard years later that they had become a Christian. Don't worry if you don't have a spectacular story to share – only God knows how our lives have influenced others for his sake.

Read: Ruth 4:13-22

Ruth had arrived in Bethlehem as a friendless, penniless, childless stranger and now, by verse 14 of chapter 4, she has become the praise of an adoring community. She's going to have a baby. 'All your concerns, Naomi, of chapter 1 have been more than answered in the providence of God. And this one who is to be born will renew your life and will sustain you in your old age because this daughter-in-law of yours, what a girl she is. She loves you and she is actually better to you than seven sons.'

'Then Naomi took the child and laid him in her lap and cared for him' (v16). It's a lovely picture. What a wonderful ending. The movie that had begun in black and white is now in glorious technicolour. The soundtrack that had been a lament is now swelling to a triumphant crescendo and Ruth, who hasn't had a speaking part since verse 17 of chapter 3, is now fading completely from view and the camera is back on Naomi. God is preoccupied with Naomi.

Let this be an encouragement to every Naomi. Through experiences of bitterness and disappointment, God is at work and Naomi, who was happy for her name to be switched to Mara, is now very happy to be called Naomi again. Wonder of all wonders, miracle of miracles, the God of the nations who is vitally involved in the personal life of this widow and her daughter-in-law, provides for her this little bundle that is now on her lap. Naomi exercises semi-parental responsibility for him, and gladly accepts the care of this little lad.

- *How has life changed for Naomi?*

But this last chapter contains far more than a lovely pastoral scene. It's far more than a family matter with limited significance. It would be a wonderful story in itself, if it ended there and it was simply a story that said, 'God is interested in the widow and in the afflicted and in the lives of ordinary people on the humdrum track of life.' That would be fine but the end of the story is so brilliant because what we have in the closing verses is a reminder of what we might refer to, in conclusion, as the mystery of history. Why else would they finish with a genealogy?

John Stott, in his book *Authentic Christianity*,[2] says, 'We must never set theology and history over against each other since Scripture refuses to do so. The history it records is salvation history and the salvation it proclaims was achieved by means of historical events.'

- *Why is the historical aspect of our faith so important?*
- *The lovely events of this story don't find their significance in the immediate impact upon the characters that we have been introduced to. God's plan is far larger than what is immediately apparent. The glories and tragedies of national events, the joys and sorrows, pains and disappointments of family life do not find their meaning ultimately within personal biography or human history. Finally, and ultimately, each event is significant in the story of redemption.*
- *What does it say about God's priorities and values that Ruth, a foreigner, and Naomi, a destitute widow, are incorporated into redemption history?*
- *Share with the group your place in redemption history, your spiritual family tree. Who told you the gospel? Who were the people involved in your conversion? Can you go further back in history; do you know who was involved in their conversion?*
- *The story of Ruth is 'far more than a family matter with limited significance.' Brainstorm all the other times in the Bible where this phrase applies. For example, sibling rivalry led Joseph's brothers to sell him to travellers but he ended up in Egypt overseeing food distribution during the famine and so preserving the Israelite nation.*

- *What difference does it make to you to know that you are playing a part in redemption history? How does it challenge your priorities, attitudes and behaviour?*

The whole story of the Bible is about getting from Genesis 12 to Revelation 7. In Genesis 12, God calls Abraham to leave his people and his father's household and to go to a land he does not know. He promises, 'I will make you into a great nation, I will bless you, I will make your name great. You will be a blessing. I will bless those who bless you. Whoever curses you I will curse and all the peoples on earth will be blessed through you.' Now the rest of the story of the Bible is getting us to Revelation chapter 7 which gives us the fulfilment, the ultimate answer of the promise of God to Abraham in Genesis chapter 12. John looks and sees a great multitude that no one could count from every nation and tribe and people and language.

If you realise that we get to Revelation 7 as a result of the promise of God in Genesis 12, then you will begin to put the big picture together. Remember at the end of the book of Judges they said 'At that time, everybody did what they wanted.' They were all doing their own thing, because they had no king. The hint is that if they had a king, everything would be super. Then you have the story of Ruth and we end with the genealogy and who's here at the end of genealogy? David, the shepherd boy who became the king. David is a man after God's own heart but he isn't perfect and when we watch him reign as king, we realise that although he fits part of the picture, he doesn't fit the total picture. He is clearly not the serpent crusher who has been promised in Genesis chapter 3. He is obviously not the great ruler from the tribe of Judah who has been mentioned in Genesis 49. There is clearly still one greater than David to come, which is made clear to him through the prophet, Nathan. In 2 Samuel 7 are these amazing words that are partially fulfilled in Solomon and are ultimately fulfilled only in Jesus who, according to Luke, in chapter 11 and verse 31, is able to put Solomon into the shadows.

- *Look up Genesis 3:15 and 49:8-12 – what evidence is there that these verses apply ultimately only to Jesus?*

'The LORD declares to you that the LORD himself will establish a house for you: When your days are over and you rest with your fathers, I will raise up your offspring to succeed you, who will come from your own body, and I will establish his kingdom. He is the one who will build a house for my Name', (that's clearly a reference to Solomon) 'and I will establish the throne of his kingdom forever.' (That's a reference that points beyond Solomon.) 'I will be his father, and he will be my son. When he does wrong', (that's also a reference to Solomon) 'I will punish him with the rod of men, with floggings inflicted by men. But my love will never be taken away from him, as I took it away from Saul, whom I removed from before you. Your house and your kingdom will endure forever before me, your throne will be established forever.' That's another reference that points beyond Solomon.

This is the challenge of doing Old Testament theology; it's like walking in the hills. If you go hillwalking and you don't know where you are, you say 'Only another few hundred yards and we're at the summit.' Then you get to the top and there's another summit. And you get there and there's another ridge to climb. That is the way that redemptive history is unfolding for us in the Old Testament. Just when we think we have the fulfilment of God's promises, we realise that they're only partially fulfilled. In the coming of this king David, all of the expectations are there but eventually we have to say that he's not the one. What we ultimately discover is that these relatively unknown, apparently insignificant lives of Ruth and Boaz are central to all that God is doing in the world. I can't improve on the commentator Atkinson's words

> Jesus' life, in terms of physical descent, was linked to the story of a Moabite girl gleaning in a barley field miles from home, to a caring mother-in-law and a loving kinsman; to a night-time conversation at the threshing floor; to the willingness of a wealthy farmer to go beyond the requirements of the law in his care for the needy. In short, it is in the ordinariness of the lives of ordinary people that God is working his purpose out.

- *Why do you think God usually chooses to work through ordinary people in the ordinariness of their lives?*
- *We are still on that journey to Revelation 7 when we will see that great multitude from all over the world praising God in heaven. How can we keep ourselves focused on this big picture perspective, rather than getting overwhelmed with the ordinary details of our lives?*

FURTHER STUDY

The book of Ruth closes with a genealogy. If we believe that 'All Scripture is God-breathed and is useful for teaching, rebuking, correcting and training in righteousness, so that the man of God may be thoroughly equipped for every good work' (2 Tim. 3:16-17) then the genealogies and the many lists in the Bible must be relevant to us. Consider 1 Chronicles 1-9, Nehemiah 3:1-32 and Matthew 1:1-17. What did these Bible records mean to the first readers and what lessons do they teach us today?

REFLECTION AND RESPONSE

In silence, consider your place in redemption history. Thank God that even in the ordinary, mundane things of life he is fulfilling his plan and purpose. Thank him for those who shared the gospel with you and pray for those in your care with whom you can share the gospel.

As a group pray that:

- As individuals you would not be overwhelmed by the ordinary details of life but entrust them to God and keep your eyes on the big picture of his salvation plan for the world.
- Your church would increase its interest in evangelism and discipleship and so play an even greater role in the history of redemption.
- The church universal would be used in a significant way to impact our generation for God and that we would be faithful to God's truth and proclaiming the gospel.

REVIEW OF THE BOOK OF RUTH

Reread the book of Ruth in one sitting.

- What is the main message of the book? Try and describe it in one sentence.
- What is the main lesson you have learnt from the book? Consider how God has challenged you. Do you need to:
  - Rethink your treatment of the poor and the outcast?
  - Ask for his help in your family relationships and dynamics?
  - Trust in his providence?
  - Trust him in your struggles?
  - Recognise his grace and favour towards you in Christ?
  - Do something else?
- The book of Ruth ends by giving us a glimpse of God's redemption plan. Consider what role you are playing in God's plan to bring salvation to the whole world. Have you got another agenda for your life or do you want to be part of God's plan? If you want to be part of this plan, what changes in your lifestyle and priorities do you need God's help with?

POINTS TO PONDER

- What have you learnt about God?
- What have you learnt about yourself?
- What actions or attitudes do you need to change as a result?

PART TWO

Introduction

Where are the leaders?

Some time ago I was reading an editorial on the nature of our heroes in *The Los Angeles Times*. 'Whatever happened to the public heroes of yesterday?' asked the journalist.

> We live in an age of spiritually timid and lacklustre men, for whom the very concept of bold leadership is an anathema. The leaders of our parents' generation battled depression, defeated fascism, secured civil rights. Ours seems to have no bigger agenda than to hang on to power. We have come to expect style and not substance from our leaders. The ugly, eloquent American, Abraham Lincoln, would never be elected today, nor in fact would he run for president, for the ills of our political system are enough to dissuade even the greatest idealists. Is it surprising then that heroic leadership is a thing of the past?

I think there is a leadership deficit in our nation and in our churches. There is a desperate need for people of all ages and all backgrounds to rise up, avoid mediocrity, claim the promises of Christ and live in power, making a difference to their communities and churches. It is my prayer that these five characters will so inspire us that we will go on to heroic leadership, wherever God might place us.

CHAPTER 11

Elijah – God's prophet on the run

Aim: To learn how to survive spiritual lows and be restored by God

FOCUS ON THE THEME

We all go through highs and lows in our spiritual lives – often corresponding to other life events. Share your deepest troughs and highest peaks with each other.

Read: 1 Kings 19:1-21

We are going to look at five steps in Elijah's life, three down and two up. We are looking at a man who is depressed, discouraged, and who feels useless. This is about heroic leadership gone wrong. King David has established the great priority of a relationship with God and after him comes Solomon, but Solomon's descendants squabble and the kingdom is divided between Rehoboam and Jeroboam – the northern and the southern kingdoms. The kingdoms, particularly the northern kingdom, had a bad set of kings for a long time. Ahab, the king in this passage, is one of the worst, a weak-kneed man dominated by a manipulative and very powerful wife. There's a clear sense in this passage that Elijah is dealing with society and culture at a depraved point in history, standing up for God when the leaders of the day claim no allegiance to Yahweh. Doesn't that strike you as being appropriate today? Very few of our political leaders claim allegiance to the Christian faith, and we long for those who are genuinely converted to be in leadership.

Elijah ministered at a time when there was no spiritual leadership coming from the politicians. His life is one of conflict, passion and power. An enormously confrontational character, he fed a starving widow and her boy, saw him raised from death and irritated the political powers by proclaiming God's kingdom wherever he could. The land was in defeat and despair. Yahweh, the one true God, was there in the hearts and minds of a few, but four hundred and fifty prophets served Baal and four hundred served Asherah.

The immediate context for our story is 1 Kings 18: Elijah defeating the prophets of Baal on Mount Carmel. Mount Carmel is about eighteen hundred feet high. Out to the east you look down to the plains going towards the northern end of the Jordan Valley and to the west you look out towards the Mediterranean. Elijah is on Mount Carmel with the prophets of Baal, with this enormous sacrifice. God says to him 'Prove once and for all my splendour.' So he bravely tells them 'You set it alight if you can. Show us that Baal is the true god.' They dance round it, and Elijah mocks them. 'Shout louder, maybe your god's deaf. Maybe he's out.' Baal doesn't answer and Elijah, in that great act of spiritual bravado, has the offering soaked in water and cries to God. Suddenly, God answers the prayer of faith, the water is licked up in the power of the flame. The prophets of Baal are defeated and a drought that's been hanging over the nation for a while comes to an end.

DOWN TO DISCOURAGEMENT

1) Running away

In 1 Kings 19 the mood could hardly be more different. Ahab rushes back to his wife and tells her. Jezebel immediately sends a message to Elijah: 'May the gods deal with me, be it ever so severely ...' In other words, 'It's my life or yours.' Many commentators have commented that Elijah has no trouble at all with four hundred and fifty male Baal prophets, and yet he is terrified of one stroppy woman; the wife of the king, whose word is law. From the incredible success of Carmel, Elijah finds himself disillusioned, running away. Verse 3: 'Elijah was afraid and ran for his life.' He headed south, out of their kingdom as rapidly as possible and left his servant in Beersheba. He even went another day's journey into the desert and sat under a juniper tree. It's a white-flowered shrub really, not so much a tree, and grew to about ten feet in height. They didn't provide much shelter in the southern desert, but they gave all the shelter there was.

Elijah huddles under this shrub and says, 'I have had enough, LORD. Take my life.' He has gone from success to suicide; from the triumph of Carmel to the desolation of the desert. It's a well-known psychological fact that there are periods of low after periods of high. That's a perfectly normal psychological response to victory.

Yet there's something more than that here. It seems to me there is the work of the enemy of souls also; a spiritual developing of that low. We often blame Satan for doing things. I rather think he's not as active in some things as we imagine he is, but I suspect he manipulated this to turn Elijah's discouragement into downright depression: 'Take my life.'

All at once an angel touched him. It's interesting that the angel simply meets his physical need to start with. Sometimes, in pastoral counselling, you are asked for profound answers to people's difficult questions. Many pastoral problems in the church would be met if people would eat correctly, exercise properly and go to bed earlier. We have got to look after our bodies because they have a significant effect on our minds. The angel says, 'Get up and eat' and made him a meal. 'The angel of the LORD came back a second time and touched him and said "Get up and eat, for the journey is too much for you." So he got up and ate and drank. Strengthened by that food, he travelled forty days and forty nights until he reached Horeb' (1 Kgs. 19:7-8). That was a total journey of around two hundred miles. It certainly needn't have taken forty days and nights: almost certainly Elijah wanders in a terrified, depressed haze. The forty days and forty nights are evocative of other Old Testament allusions to forty days and forty nights, and it says in verse 9; 'There he went into a cave.' The Hebrew actually says 'and there he went into the cave'. This may be a hint that the cleft in the rock where God met Moses is precisely the place on Horeb where Elijah has an encounter with the living God. We are not entirely sure. Anyway, after victory depression sets in and Elijah is running away from God.

- *Spiritual lows inevitably follow spiritual highs because we can't maintain a mountain-top experience forever. What practical steps can we take to prevent these lows descending into spiritual discouragement and depression?*

2) *Being in the wrong place*

The second step down is in the next few verses: 'The word of the LORD came to him "What are you doing here Elijah?"'(1 Kgs. 19:9b). 'What on earth are you doing, Elijah, running away from me, in this desert place, far from the action, miles from where I want you to be confronting the sin of Ahab and Jezebel?' God's call to Elijah comes with both confrontation and compassion.

Sometimes we get into bad places, spiritually. For some it's a result of sin and God comes with stern words. 'What on earth are you doing in this place, rebelling against me?' Sometimes it's because of circumstances, pain and hurt, and God whispers in compassion, 'What are you doing here? I long for you to be restored and sent back to glory and to blessing.'

- *What are the tell-tale signs that you are in the wrong place spiritually?*

3) Being alone

There is a third step down into despair, and it's found in Elijah's isolationism. His reply to this question is the same in verses 10:14. 'He replied, "I have been very zealous for the LORD God Almighty. The Israelites have rejected your covenant, broken down your altars, and put your prophets to death with the sword. I am the only one left, and now they are trying to kill me too."'

These three states of discouragement are common in human experience: great victories and then running away from God into depression and discouragement, then being in the wrong place spiritually and thirdly blaming everybody else for things that go wrong. If you've got someone in your church who is in the wrong place spiritually they're not going to be positive, because when we are in the wrong place vertically with God, our horizontal relationships are always soured, and we become bitter and self-centred, just like Elijah.

'God, I'll tell you what I'm doing here. I'm here because I tried to be your faithful servant and all those other wretched Israelites' – the word 'wretched' is not in the original Hebrew here, but it is clearly implied – 'have rejected your covenant and broken down your altars. They are not involved in your law or your worship, and they put your messengers to death. These are your people.'

Elijah's blaming God and everybody else. When we get into the wrong place, we blame God and everybody else for what's gone wrong in our lives. We have to take responsibility for where we are.

God recognises that often we get tired after a lifetime of Christian service. After a series of victories we're burnt out, running away from God, in the wrong place, blaming God and everybody else for our problems. Into that setting, Elijah begins the two steps upward into restoration, recovery and renewal.

RESTORATION, RECOVERY AND RENEWAL

'Go out,' verse 11 says 'and stand on the mountain in the presence of the LORD, for the LORD is about to pass by. Then a great and powerful wind tore the mountains apart and shattered the rocks before the LORD, but the LORD was not in the wind' (1 Kgs 19:11b) nor was he in the earthquake or the fire. But 'after the fire came a gentle whisper.' The nearest translation of this Hebrew phrase is the Paul Simon song; *The sound of silence* is the nearest translation. After this spectacular show, there is the sound of silence, a still small whisper.

God is in the spectacular sometimes, but those who are hungry to experience God must learn to recognise him in the ordinary as well as in the spectacular. Most of us spend most of our lives doing very ordinary things. Whatever we claim to experience of God, and it is marvellous to seek him for experiences old and new, we have to live out the God-life as we eat, sleep and drink, and raise children, go to work and do the ordinary things of life. God wants to be in the normal as well as the extra-normal, in the natural as well as in the supernatural. There is a great danger when we relegate God only to the so-called miraculous. God wants to be involved in every day of our lives.

- *How can we learn to recognise God in the ordinary aspects of our lives?*

1) Go back

God is in the gentle whisper, and what does God say to Elijah? 'Go back the way you came.' For many of us the only way back to God is to go back home. We want to move on, to new things. We want to live out the Christian faith in different climates, different contexts. We think 'How easy things would have been, if only we lived in a different country, or went to a different church, or were married to a different woman or could have chosen our parents.'

'Go back the way you came.' The way up from the depression, the bottom place so many of us find ourselves in, is to run towards the living God.

- *What value does 'going back' have? How does it help the process of spiritual restoration?*
- *To make spiritual progress sometimes it is appropriate to go back. At other times we need to move on, to a new church, a new set of friends or new circumstances. How can we discern which is right in a given situation?*

2) A new commission

God gives Elijah a new commissioning to serve him again. He says, 'I haven't finished with you. Go back north. I'm going to give you a message that will shake the people around you.' First of all he gives him an international ministry. 'Go to Syria.' It's another country. 'Then anoint a king over Israel.' That's a national ministry. Then 'Anoint Elisha.' That's a local spiritual ministry. Suddenly, Elijah goes from being nothing to being given an international, a national and a local ministry, all in one verse.

God must really want to use him, and he isn't going to leave Elijah on his own. Part of Elijah's depression is that he is a solitary agent. He works on his own. He is isolated, so Satan picks him off relatively easily. God gives him a new companion, Elisha.

If I've learnt anything in twenty years of pastoral ministry, it's that we desperately need God and we desperately need other Christians. We need to hold each other accountable for our spiritual lives and to love one another. A friendless Christian is a Christian on the way to backsliding. If only there was someone for him to mentor and invest his life in, someone to cheer him up when he felt down, someone to come alongside him. God knew that Elijah needed more than a new commissioning and anointing. He needed the friendship of a fellow worker. Some of the depression in our churches, particularly among leaders, is because they are isolated: alone and unaccountable for their activity. They have no one who will look them in the eye, only leadership teams whom they hold at arm's length. They never open their souls to another human being. So the church is littered with broken, depressed, defeated leaders; pastors who are giving up, moving out of ministry because they can no longer cope with the demands of the church, the world, family and all those things crowding in on them. There are Christians who feel like giving up their faith. They have been damaged by the church, they're fed up with the way their lives are going and they cry to God for a new commissioning, a new friend, a new partner in the gospel.

Find a prayer partner, find a colleague, build yourself into a team. The answer to much discouragement is team, fellowship and friendship.

- *Why has faith become so individualised in the West?*
- *How can Christian friendship deepen to become fellowship? Look at how David, Jesus and Paul sought and found fellowship from their friends in 1 Samuel 23:15-18, Matthew 26:36-37 and Colossians 4:7-11.*
- *How can we ensure our faith is encouraged but not dependent on the accountability and support of others?*

God also reminds Elijah that he's been wrong all along about being alone. I don't know whether you've noticed, but when people are livid, it's not the best time for a rational discussion. Neither is it the best time when you are in the pit of despair. Sometimes people are deeply discouraged and you want to say to them, 'This is ridiculous. Here are five reasons why you ought not to be so fed up.' Those logical reasons don't penetrate the depressive haze. We just can't take it in. We want to take in that God wants to use us, but we can't.

One of the great pastoral blessings is to care for people in crisis. Less than two weeks ago, I officiated at the funeral of a twenty-five-year-old who had Downs Syndrome, a son of our associate minister at the church. He knows all the reasons for the death in his head, but where are the answers in the heart? The logical, clever, theological explanations are all true, but they are not necessarily felt. The time comes when silence is the best argument. Some people in your church, who are depressed, discouraged and broken, don't need three reasons to get better; they need a loving arm around the shoulder. Later they'll need the arguments; right now they need the love.

Notice how God deals with Elijah. He doesn't shout at him in the wilderness, through the angel: 'Elijah, you are a wimp. You have just defeated all these prophets. Get back there right now.' God meets his need. Elijah is fed and watered. God sends him back and gives him a new commissioning. He explains to him that he's not finished with him. 'Elijah, I know you're fed up, I know you're afraid, I know you're running away, I know you're exhausted, I know you're suicidal even. I know you are angry with me and angry with God's people. I know you're in the wrong place geographically and spiritually. But I haven't finished with you. You're going to go to Syria to change the shape of that nation, and you're going to go back to Israel to change the shape of your own nation.

When Elijah is thrilled with the new commissioning, then God says to him, by way of encouragement, 'I've got seven thousand in Israel who haven't bowed the knee to Baal and whose mouths have not kissed him.' That was a typical Middle Eastern way of worship, to kiss the head or toe of an idol as a sign of worship. God gently reminds Elijah, when he's up to hearing it, that not only is he not the only one, there are seven thousand who haven't bowed the knee. Elijah's eyes are opened, and he can somehow see again, with less jaundiced eyes, that there is a God, that he is doing his work, and that the people of God, for all their failings – it was still true they were breaking down the altars, it was still true they were disregarding the covenant – but still there were those who loved God, who wanted to serve him and follow him. Cynicism about God's people is a terrible disease. Of course the church is in a mess. But God says, 'You might think you're the only one left, the only one who's sound and strong, who really cares. But I tell you, hidden in the great morass of the spiritual nation are thousands who haven't bowed the knee to Baal, who love me and who want to serve me and follow me, and who want to go on being my servants.'

Then 1 Kings 19 and the rest of the chapter talks about the call of Elisha and a range of other miracle stories follow on in 1 Kings 20 and following. The story continues to get exciting. But right at the heart of the Elijah narrative is this story about three steps down to discouragement and depression, and then two up to redemption and restoration. God hasn't finished with you yet. That's the message of Elijah. There's a new commissioning, a new anointing, a new call and a new helper God wants to bring alongside you.

- *'God hasn't finished with you yet.' How has God shown you this recently? What new role or call has he given you, what fresh experience of God have you had, what aspect of your character have you sensed him beginning to work on, what new burdens for prayer do you have? If you don't sense God working in your life right now pray that he will reveal himself to you.*

FURTHER STUDY

Jonah was another prophet who ran away from God and from his new commission. He didn't want to preach repentance to the wicked Ninevites in case they obeyed and God forgave them. So he got on a boat and headed for Tarshish, fleeing in the opposite direction of God's call. Take time to read the book of Jonah: how were Jonah and Elijah's experiences of spiritual depression similar? How did God deal with this prophet and what was the process of restoration for Jonah? What particular lessons can you to learn from this book and this reluctant prophet?

REFLECTION AND RESPONSE

Circle where you are on the scale of

depression-discouragement-redemption-recovery-restoration

- Are you running away from God?
- Are you in the wrong place spiritually because of sin or hurt?
- In your bitterness, are you becoming self-centred, blaming everyone else for the wrong in your life?
- Do you need to recognise God in the ordinary?
- Do you need to go back and deal with situations and people from your past?
- Do you need to accept God's commission and new anointing?
- Do you need to develop an accountability or mentoring relationship?

If it is appropriate, share with another member of the group how God has challenged or encouraged you from this study. Spend time praying for each other. During the week, email or phone each other with prayer requests, answers to prayer and updates on your situation.

POINTS TO PONDER

- What have you learnt about God?
- What have you learnt about yourself?
- What actions or attitudes do you need to change as a result?

CHAPTER 12

Samson – Passion and power out of control

Aim: To recognise our weakness and God's strength

FOCUS ON THE THEME

Consider your character. What are your top three strengths and weaknesses? Have your strengths and weaknesses changed as you have grown older or are you just more aware of them? If you know the other members of the group well, perhaps you could discuss your list with them and see if they agree with you.

How often do we use God's strength to deal with our character flaws? Or are we like Samson, allowing our weaknesses to magnify and control us?

Read: Judges 16:4-22

INTRODUCTION

Let me introduce Judges 13-16 to you, and set it in context. We're going to take highlights from the life of Samson and try to learn about this influential judge in Israel. Much of what we will say will focus on the Samson and Delilah story, but not exclusively, because to understand this incredibly enigmatic figure, we are going to have to understand a bit about his birth, and his life prior to the hair-cutting incident and the Philistines coming to capture him.

1) The days of Samson

In the great sweep of Old Testament history, we're moving back from the days of Elijah and the kings of Israel and Judah, back in time to a wilder, less organised, less controlled society. Almost all the books of the Bible make clear the Israelites moved towards God and away from him with boring monotony. They didn't seem able to sustain spirituality for a long period. The whole Old Testament is a kind of cyclical review of people moving towards God, away from him and then back to him again after a period of judgment and repentance.

In this part of their history, life is rough. The nation of Israel is not a settled coherent state with well-established ways of operating: that doesn't come until quite a bit later in the Old Testament. The book of Judges reveals God's leaders to be a series of characters that were a combination of military leader, judge, law-giver, civil authority figure or some kind of prophetic figure. It's very difficult to pin the judges down and that's particularly true of Samson. What kind of person was he? When you read about him you see that he wasn't exactly a peace-loving normal person and yet he's God's chosen instrument to begin the process of destroying the Israelites' enemies and moving towards a more settled society. God is using Samson even though he's most unlikely material.

2) The birth of Samson

Judges 13 tells us about the birth of this enigmatic character.

> Again the Israelites did evil in the eyes of the LORD, so the LORD delivered them into the hands of the Philistines for forty years. A certain man of Zorah … had a wife who was sterile and remained childless. The angel of the LORD appeared to her and said 'You are sterile and childless but you are going to conceive and have a son.'

There are interesting echoes here of a number of other angelic visitations to women throughout the Bible. You will be aware of the Abraham and Sarah story and her barrenness, which ultimately resulted in a child. And although the Virgin Mary is never described as barren and childless, an angelic visitation came to her in Luke's gospel, and Jesus, Saviour of the world, was the result. Angels arriving and babies arriving seem clearly linked in the pages of the Bible. This woman is not named. She is mentioned nineteen times in these early chapters of Samson's story but only the man is named. They discover that the curse of barrenness, which is how it was seen in Old Testament times, is alleviated by this incredible gift.

3) An ideal start

Samson had the most ideal start to his life and career. There is an angelic announcement, a miraculous birth to a barren woman, and two parents who are so determined to do what God wanted, they ask for a second visitation from the angel for help in raising their son. Perhaps this prayer, Judges 13:8, ought to be prayed by every potential parent and all of us whose children are growing or even have grown.

'O LORD, teach us how to bring up this child.' We know that the responsibility of parenthood is a significant one, and we neglect it at our peril. We know that if we abandon our children simply to the mercies of the school, or the club or their peer group, in the end they won't be those who love, follow and serve Jesus. So bad are we as a church in this nation, so failing in our Christian impact, we can't even keep our own children, let alone recruit new ones. I say that not as a word of condemnation to parents, as you'll see in a moment. Our commitment is to cry, with Samson's parents, 'God help us raise these children in ways that you want them to be raised.'

But notice that although it's every parent's responsibility to pray the prayer of Samson's parents, Samson perpetually disappointed them. He asked them, initially, to find him a wife. They were very disappointed with his choice. He often ignored them and his life in the moral realm was almost permanently an abject failure. All that his parents had invested in him, all that fabulous opportunity at the start of his life, seems to end up in murder, adultery and the visiting of prostitutes. His was a character out of control.

It's a reminder to us that even though some of us have prayed the prayer of Samson's parents, our children sometimes grow up to be very different from what we would like them to be. It breaks Christian parents' hearts all over the world and yet that tragedy occurred even here in the pages of Scripture. Even when we have done our best, our children are responsible people who must make their own decisions. Sometimes we beat ourselves with false guilt when our children stray off the path. We worry, 'What did I do wrong?' We may have done things wrong but often Christian parents are simply faced with a child choosing something else, as they have a right to do. Samson's parents would have understood something of the pain that many parents feel.

- *How has becoming a parent revealed the weaknesses in your character? If you don't have children, consider what particular situations have highlighted your character flaws most.*

- *How has parenting or the situation you described above helped you learn to rely on God's strength?*

4) Who's in control?

Samson lives a life in which his appetites, not God are in control. In chapter 14 he says, 'Get me a Philistine woman for a wife, even though I shouldn't be marrying this woman from our enemies.' Verses 3 and 4 show that his parents are appalled at the terrible betrayal of his Judaism. Then in verse 5, 'suddenly a young lion came roaring towards him' and the Spirit of God gives him incredible power to tear the lion apart. Then as the bridegroom he hosts a feast, tells the guests a riddle, verse 12 following, but his wife can't guess the riddle so she weeps and pleads for her life. The upshot is that his wife is given to a friend and in chapter 15 he seeks revenge on the Philistines by tying three hundred foxes together and then killing people with the jawbone of an ass. Then in Chapter 16 you've got the story of Samson and Delilah.

Here is a man whose appetites are out of control. One minute he's killing Philistines with a jawbone of a mule in a kind of bloodbath frenzy of temper, the next minute he's storming off with the town gates, up a mountain, he's so angry. Is this the kind of man you would want on your church council or as a deacon? Probably not. Here's a man whose temper, drinking and womanising habits are not under control. He is not a nice man. He's a man out of control; his habits are dominating and controlling him. It's a tragedy in the making.

I don't think the problem with Samson was fundamentally sexual. Samson is simply not able to control himself. He is without equal in his ability to be the recipient of the power of the Lord, but his character is out of control.

This man fits our modern culture enormously in the expression of our appetites. If we feel something, we indulge it. There's all the psychological stuff about not repressing your feelings. Then there's the philosophical stream, birthed in some of the existentialists, culminating in the Nike slogan 'Just do it!' I grew up as a teenager in the 1960s and was told 'If it feels good, do it.' My grandparents' generation used to say things like, 'You have to learn to control yourself.' A hundred years ago, Christians and non-Christians would say, 'You must control your appetites.' Our culture says, 'You must express your appetites.' It's a vastly different scene now and Samson lives in that scene. He expresses himself with passion and energy. No appetite is too depraved for him to get involved in, no excess too much. Everything he does, even killing Philistines, which on the whole was thought to be a pretty good thing, he has to do to excess.

5) Character

Tony Blair, when asked what was the most important thing before the last election, said 'Education, education, education.' What it takes to be a good Christian leader? Character, character, character. Power is essential but without character, the fruit of that leadership is very shortlived. I think it was Peter Kusmic who first said that, 'Charisma without character is not credible.' People simply don't relate, in the long term, to a leader whose character is not transformed by the living God. Samson judged for twenty years, and he was a significant leader in many ways. But his character was his failing and it was ultimately the problem which led to his defeat. There was a fatal flaw in Samson. From a very young man, his appetites were never under control and he reaped the fruit of that in his later years.

From this Old Testament figure, God helps us to see that character flaws in our youth, if not dealt with, become giants in our middle and older age. Our Achilles heel is an appetite out of control. It might be for food, status, attention, money, fame or sexual indulgence. It might be for anything, but if our appetites are not controlled by the Spirit of God, we will ultimately explode in a mess in God's kingdom.

- *What is our role and what is God's role in transforming our character?*
- *What situations, relationships and practices should we build into our lives so that our character is transformed?*

6) The source of Samson's power

What is the source of Samson's power? Both Delilah and Samson think the source of Samson's power is his hair. But it's quite important to understand that the source of Samson's power is not, fundamentally, his hair, despite the way the story seems to unfold. If you look through the story from Chapter 13 onwards, you will notice that whenever a miracle occurs, his hair is not mentioned. Look at Judges 14:6, the lion incident: 'The Spirit of the LORD came upon him in power, so he tore the lion apart with his bare hands.' Then chapter 15:14, he's bound by ropes and about to be handed over to the Philistines: 'The Spirit of the LORD came upon him in power' and the ropes dropped from his arms, he grabbed the jaw bone of a donkey and struck a thousand men. Many of the great feats that Samson accomplished are clearly linked with the Spirit of the Lord.

Samson's Nazirite vow was characterised by three external signs:

- Do not drink wine or strong drink
- Stay away from dead bodies
- Do not let a razor touch your hair.

You might imagine therefore that the source of Samson's strength was his Nazirite vow. But he'd already abandoned most of the vow. Avoiding wine and strong drink – he wasn't doing that at all the weddings and festivals he went to. Staying away from dead bodies – how you do that while you're killing a thousand Philistines with a donkey's jawbone? Samson's completely failed two out of three forms of the Nazirite vow.

In the Delilah story Samson, undone by this character flaw, finally caves in to her pleading, and his hair is cut off. The third and final sign of the Nazirite power is gone. But the power is not really in the hair, and it's clear that that's true with the most tragic verse in the whole of Judges, in Chapter 16:20 'Then she called "Samson, the Philistines are upon you!"' She'd shaved his head 'and he awoke from his sleep and thought "I'll go out as before and shake myself free."' This is the tragedy, 'But he did not know that the LORD had left him.' Notice, it doesn't say, 'He did not know he'd just had a haircut.' The sign was not the significant issue. The sign was simply the residue of God's call on his life, and it was the final straw where God abandoned him to his fate. As the final form of his power fell away from him, God abandoned him to his fate, temporarily.

This is crucial because, although in the Old Testament form and reality, symbol and substance, are very close together. Even in the Old Testament times, the writers knew that, ultimately behind the symbol, the reality was of God's touch on our lives and that form should not be substituted for reality.

- *Can God's power leave individual Christians and churches today? If so, why and is the removal of power temporary or permanent?*

7) Where does the power come from?

The mistake Samson and Delilah made has been made by churches and Christians down the centuries. We argue in our churches about form, not about reality. We believe that when God blesses, certain things happen, and we may well be right. Some of us of a conservative evangelical persuasion are committed to the truth of the Bible and we wave it round like an icon everywhere. We are proud that our Bible is bigger, thicker, heavier. We open it, we read it, we display it everywhere. But I tell you, I've been in churches that say they honour the Bible and it's all form and no substance. We want God to come in to our churches, so we assume we'll sing a few contemporary songs. Those of us with more charismatic inclinations imagine if we raise our arms in worship, God will come. It is possible that when God comes some of us may want to raise our arms in worship, but we must never confuse form and reality.

The power's not in the hair or the order of service or in the time of the service. The power's not in whether you raise your hands or not. The power's not in the structure or programme. The power's not in some new development that comes to our churches. The crying need of our churches, my crying need, is not a new programme or a new skill. It's the Spirit of God. It was the crying need for Samson to understand. The hair was simply a remnant of a past blessing. It was a token of what God honoured but it wasn't the real thing. It was a sign of the reality. We are obsessed in our churches with form, sign and structure. That's what we argue about all the time. God forgive us. The world goes to hell around us while we argue about how many songs should be sung, whether the service is too long or too short, or whether we should have drums or an organ. What is wrong with us in the Church? We constantly mistake form for reality.

We also ought to note that Samson's name comes up again in Hebrews 11:32. He's mentioned with a list of famous saints. He only gets a very brief passing mention, and yet he's mentioned. 'What more shall I say? I do not have time to tell you about Gideon and Barak and Samson and others who through faith conquered kingdoms, administered justice, and gained what was promised; who shut the mouths of lions' and so on. He's in the hall of fame.

He'd never make it onto the leadership team of your church, would he? He wouldn't make it into our church membership, never mind into our church leadership. Yet, without for one moment condoning this man's out-of-control appetites, Samson is still used by God. I find that so encouraging. It is of course not an encouragement to sin. But it is an encouragement to realise that in my failure and my sin, God still wants to use me. This out-of-control man still finds himself in the Israelite hall of fame. Praise God for that.

- *Consider your own church – in what ways are you mistaking form for reality? What forms and structures are you protecting, assuming they guarantee God's blessing?*

8) God's strength and Samson's weakness

The story ends after the Delilah incident with Samson at his most humiliated and in those moments God still uses him. His eyes are put out in a horrific incident; he's taken away by the Philistines and brought out, perhaps some years or months later, as a figure of fun at a Philistine carnival. There he is, in that great immortal phrase of John Milton's, 'eyeless in Gaza'. Again, the power's not in the hair because he realises he has come back to this God. As they praise Dagon, Samson gets angry. He cries out, 'O Sovereign LORD, remember me. O God, please, strengthen me just once more.' It wasn't because his hair had grown back that he was able to do this final act, but because God strengthened him to be able to do it. 'With one blow I will get revenge on the Philistines for my two eyes.' It's not a particularly godly motive, the motive of revenge, and yet the writer reminds us that he killed more people in his death than he had in the whole of his life. That was quite significant, because the Philistines with their god Dagon dominated this part of the ancient world. The Philistines thought that their god was going to take over the whole community and Yahweh would be squeezed out. It's quite symbolic that Samson, as a picture of the whole of Israel, crushes the mighty Dagon in his death throes as the pillars are broken and Samson causes the temple to fall.

When does God use him? Again this is a moment, for me, of enormous encouragement. Samson is an enigmatic character. I can't understand quite why he's included in the pages of the Old Testament. I would much prefer God to use nicer people. But no, God takes this eyeless, broken, shattered figure of fun, a parody of himself, a shadow of that great mountain of a man who strode around womanising, tearing gates off cities and striking fear into the hearts of the Philistines. He's a nothing, and at the point of his nothingness he does more than he did in all his somethingness.

The great thing about the Samson story is it's a lesson about what not to do. It's a lesson not to rely on human ingenuity, strength and skill, and not to rely on religious tokens but to rely wholly on the Spirit of God. It's a lesson, too, that when we are at our most broken, defeated and despairing and feel all hope is gone, it is precisely at that moment that God is able to restore and raise us up. Isn't that fantastic? At our deepest, darkest moment, God can use us. Samson is a great illustration of horror, of failure, of awfulness. In his dark moments – and he's not just dark spiritually, he's literally dark, he can't see – God's light bursts in for one final time in a revelation in this power encounter. Given Dagon on the one hand and Yahweh on the other, there is no contest in God's mind. Dagon must fall, the Philistines must be crushed and defeated, and that rout was to go on for many years until, ultimately, King David comes, mops up most of the remains and establishes his authority.

Samson begins so well, and ends with a glimmer of light, but most of the years in between are disastrous in terms of his character and behaviour. We remind ourselves that whatever the miraculous start, it's the continuing of the journey with God which is crucial. We remind ourselves of the fatal flaw in Samson, and that any appetite out of control will be the undoing of us too. We remind ourselves that it's not the form that matters, but the power of the Spirit of God. We remind ourselves that in the moment of degradation, when we feel utterly broken, God can use us more in our emptiness than he can when we're full of ourselves.

- *Why does God use us most when we are empty and broken? Look up the following verses to start your discussion – John 12: 23-26, 1 Corinthians 1:26-2:5, 2 Corinthians 4:7-11, 12:7-10.*
- *Consider the older Christians you know. How have they managed to continue the journey of faith well and what lessons can you learn from them?*
- *Given Samson's flaws, why do you think God used him? What encouragements, lessons and challenges are there for us in this account?*

FURTHER STUDY

Like many of us, Samson's parents no doubt experienced both the joys and the sorrows of parenthood. Look up in a concordance the words 'child', 'children' and 'son'. What does the Bible tell us about our role and responsibilities as parents? Discuss what the Bible teaches with your spouse or prayer partner – in what practical ways can you implement these biblical instructions?

REFLECTION AND RESPONSE

In silence, consider your own character again:

- To what extent are you allowing your character to be transformed by the living God?
- What character flaws do you need to deal with?
- What appetites do you need to bring under God's control?
- What decisions, changes or choices do you need to make as a result of this study?

When Samson was aware of his weakness and his reliance on God's strength, God used him more powerfully than ever before. In twos, pray that God would use you – at work, at home, at school, at university, in the church. Pray for each other that in your daily life you would learn to listen to God's Spirit and rely on his strength.

POINTS TO PONDER

- What have you learnt about God?
- What have you learnt about yourself?
- What actions or attitudes do you need to change as a result?

CHAPTER 13

Deborah – A woman of courage and conviction

Aim: To examine some of the key qualities of a leader

FOCUS ON THE THEME

What makes a good leader? Invite the group members to finish this sentence – 'A leader is someone who ... ' Discuss the specific character qualities of a leader in politics, business and on the social circuit. Do we admire the same traits in our Christian leaders or do we recognise and promote unique character qualities?

Read: Judges 4:1-24

INTRODUCTION

Deborah is one of the very few significant female leaders in the Old Testament. One fact is certain. Whatever your view on the subject of women in leadership, you can accept this as completely true: Deborah was a woman. It's quite important to be clear about that statement as we unpack what God seems to be saying today to the church, through his word. I'm conscious that in talking about a woman leader, the ice on which I skate is thin, as there is an enormous diversity of views about the role of women in marriage, in the church and in society. There are extreme viewpoints on the role of women held within the church. There are those who believe that a woman's place is in the home, and that's a view at one end of the spectrum. At the other end, there's Gloria Steinem's evocative phrase, 'A woman without a man is like a fish without a bicycle.' I also like this quotation from Rebecca West, one of the early feminists: 'There is, of course, no reason for the existence of the male sex, except that one sometimes needs help in moving the piano.'

You will have heard that men are becoming increasingly irrelevant to the procreative process. That statement has huge ethical implications. The role and relationship of the two genders, inside the church and out of it, is fraught with complexity and difficulty. The relationship between men and women and the way it's perceived in society have changed enormously in the last fifty years and the preaching of the word doesn't come into a vacuum. We've changed and our culture's changed. Yet into that changing world the timeless unchanging truths of the Bible are revealed. That's the great miracle. In fact, the femaleness of Deborah is not the prime point I want to make, although that's going to have to be the starting point because it is clearly a contentious and important issue. But the issues in this passage are related to leadership, not fundamentally to female leadership.

- *How have the roles of men and women changed in the last fifty years? What difference has this made to the nature of leadership in our society?*

BACKGROUND

The world of the Judges was an enormously turbulent Wild West kind of environment. Joshua had left behind a broadly subdued land but the tribes were not welded together into a nation state; that didn't happen until David's time. Israel is struggling to find a national identity: twelve tribes at odds with each other and with the pagan nations around them. These thirteen or so judges ministered over a period of roughly two hundred years, about one thousand years before Christ.

Judges 1 and the first part of Judges 2 are really a kind of summary of where the nation's got to in the immediate aftermath of Joshua's death. In Chapter 3 we read about Othniel, the first of the judges; Ehud, the second of the judges and Shamgar, who may not have been a judge at all but simply a mighty warrior. Deborah is either the third or the fourth judge. Each of these judges is introduced with a kind of literary device, found for the first time in Chapter 3:7: 'The Israelites did evil in the eyes of the LORD.' You see the recurring pattern through this piece of literature. The Israelites do evil, God raises up a judge to bring them back to himself, the Israelites do evil, God raises up a judge and so on. Into that maelstrom of rebellion, God raises up Deborah.

DESPERATE TIMES FOR ISRAEL

In Judges 4:3, notice these chariots, Sisera's army had cruelly oppressed the Israelites for twenty years. They cried to the Lord for help. This is not a monthly oppression, or six months of difficulty. This is a desperate period in Israelite history. The third judge is dealing with over twenty years of cruel oppression. And we're on the cusp of the change between the Bronze Age and the Iron Age, when foot soldiers were increasingly giving way to the brutality of the iron chariot. Chariots could take out dozens of men, because they were enormous, lethal things. The Israelites only had access to numbers of men. They were largely a nomadic people and had not acquired the sophisticated war weaponry of the settled peoples of which Jabin was king. So in Judges 4 you have the Israelites, really mountain warriors in the deserts, moving very quickly but not able to cope with the incredible power of nine hundred iron chariots.

Into that mix comes Deborah, capable both of wise counsel and decisive action. She was married to a man called Lappidoth, of whom we know nothing apart from the fact that he was the husband of Deborah. She seems to have been judging Israel at that time, holding court under the Palm of Deborah, which appears to be an enormous tree, presumably providing shade. People came to her for wisdom of various kinds.

She sent for Barak, the captain of her host. Barak seems to be a basically good man but a little slow on the uptake. She says, 'Go, take with you ten thousand men of Naphtali and Zebulun and lead the way to Mount Tabor. I will lure Sisera, the commander of Jabin's army, with his chariots and troops to the Kishon River and give him into your hands.' This is going to be a significant military strategy. Barak says, 'Please Deborah, come and hold my hand' but I think it's actually more about him wanting a guarantee of God's presence in the battle. 'Very well,' said Deborah, 'I will come with you, but if I do the honour will go to a woman.' It sounds like she means herself, but it transpires some other woman is going to get the glory. Deborah went with him and the ten thousand men followed him, and when they got to the Kishon River, Barak advances on the army, the army is routed and Sisera abandons his chariot and flees on foot.

Judges 5 gives us the commentary and seems to imply that as the chariots came down towards the Kishon River God arranged thunder and lightning and a flash flood. The Kishon River overflowed its banks, the heavy chariots got bogged down in the flood plain around the river and were useless. Ten thousand light infantry men were far more effective than nine hundred iron chariots sinking slowly into a muddy flood plain.

This is not an uncommon military strategy. The Americans struggled in Vietnam for years because although they had far greater firepower in every way, the Vietcong knew their way around the jungles. The Russians in Afghanistan were totally unable to rout the mujaheddin, because they were light travellers. They were greater in terms of tank power and plane power, but the mujaheddin hid in the mountains and would just disappear. This form of warfare is not uncommon: the light infantry defeat the heavy tanks on a muddy plain.

THE DEATH OF SISERA

They all fell and were killed. They were in heavy armour, and maybe they were thrown from their chariots: whatever happened, there was devastation. However, chapter 4:17 says, 'Sisera ... came to the tent of Jael, the wife of Heber the Kenite.' He probably thought he was safe, because the Kenites and the Israelites had a fractious relationship. What he didn't know was peace had been brokered between the Kenites and the Israelites. He goes into the tent and asks for water. It was most unusual in the ancient world for a man to be alone with a woman other than his wife, but he must have been desperate. I don't know where the men were, perhaps they were out with their flocks. She gives him what is called a 'skin' of milk, a kind of fermented milk which would taste slightly soured, but had an alcoholic dimension. Maybe he was both exhausted and slightly drugged. Either way he must have been sleeping heavily, because I think I would notice if someone was trying to drive a tent peg through my temple, however tired I was. And so he dies.

Barak, in hot pursuit of Sisera, arrives and Jael says, 'Come on in, I'll show you the man you're looking for.' To his complete amazement the prophecy of Deborah comes true and the actual final nail in the coffin, the final tent peg in the temple, is administered by Jael. 'On that day God subdued Jabin.' He was totally broken by this conflict, verse 23, 'the hand of the Israelites grew stronger and stronger against Jabin the Canaanite king until they destroyed him.' This wasn't the end of the battling, but it was the pivotal fundamental battle.

Almost all war historians describe battles in both 1917/18 and 1944/45 as 'the pivotal battle'. This is one of those moments in human history when, although sporadic fighting followed, nevertheless at this point the back of Canaanite power was clearly, effectively broken. After that there was a mopping-up operation, several more months of war, but the enemy was defeated.

WHERE ARE THE LEADERS?

I've taken quite a long time to spell out that background, because it is important that we do Scripture justice and understand what is actually being recorded here. Firstly, I'm going to make a number of points about leadership. Desperate times demand courageous leaders. Timeserving functionary bureaucrats might be all right for peacetime, but in wartime you need dynamic, God-filled leaders of extraordinary passion, vision and courage. I am pleased to tell you that in the line of these thirteen judges, God saw fit to raise up a woman called Deborah to be the passionate, visionary, courageous leader these crisis times needed.

We are living in desperate, crisis times. All the statistics show the church of Jesus in Great Britain is in terminal decline. The number of people who read their Bibles every day, or who are growing in discipleship, is in free-fall. We are in a desperate state in the church, and we need to pray that godly men and women will be raised up with courage to speak God's word powerfully. Not the mealy-mouthed person who will just get by, but the man or woman who will pay whatever price it takes to speak out for God, however they are criticised outside the church and, tragically, inside it.

Why do I think Deborah was a woman of courage? Well, because she was a woman. In the ancient world, having a woman in leadership was unusual. Very few women rose to the kind of prominence which is accorded to Deborah. If you are in an oppressed group, as women certainly were in the Middle East, and still are today, if you are going to lead from that background, you'd better have the courage of your convictions.

The church of Jesus in Britain has oppressed a whole series of groups in the last hundred years, and we ought to be ashamed of ourselves. We have not seen working-class people released into leadership in our middle-class churches. Where are the black faces in our congregations, and where are the women that God has called and gifted? I know that there are different views on women in leadership, and we all claim biblical support for those views. Some of you will feel that there is no ministry from which women are excluded in the church. Others will feel, and you will base this on passages in Corinthians and Timothy, that women should be excluded from pastoral charge, or from eldership, or from a teaching ministry and so on. That's a perfectly biblical viewpoint. But we have to remember there are godly, conservative, Bible believing, evangelical Christians who have different views from us, and frankly, we are in no state to muck about on the edges of these issues. There's a world out there going to hell while we argue whether women can take the offering. We are sick. There's something wrong with us that our priorities are so distorted.

How dare we, in the last century, send women all over the world into the worst possible situations and environments, telling them to go and conquer lands where no man has gone, preaching, planting churches, caring for people, and when we bring them back home the best we can do for them is to get them to join the tea committee? It's obscene. It cannot be justified by any biblical interpretation. It's perfectly appropriate that our view of Scripture demands women be excluded from certain offices. We can agree among ourselves to disagree. But the reality is still, in general terms, that we aren't giving the liberty and the opportunity to women, to people of different colour, race, class or background. 'All one in Christ Jesus' has been a mockery in many of our churches and we have missed the opportunity to see significant gifts and ministry released.

- *Given the state of crisis in the church and your own local context, what are the gifts, ministries and leadership qualities you believe the church needs to cultivate?*

LEADERS OF COURAGE

God raised Deborah up. It took courage to be a woman in leadership. It takes courage now to be a leader of any kind, if you're going to be a good one. God needs to raise up the Deborahs who will rise above their background, their gender restrictions, their circumstances, the cultural constraints that bind them, and say 'God, if you call me I'm here. I'll go for you, I'll do it.' There is so much fear in Christian leadership. Pray for your pastor and for the leaders in your church. Ask God to help them be more afraid of him than they are of you.

In Nehemiah 13:25 in the *Living Bible*, you see a leader with real courage. The people of God in Nehemiah's time were marrying people from other tribes and other religions. Nehemiah calls them together and 13:25 of the *Living Bible* says, 'I punched some of them, and I pulled out their hair.' Then, after he'd punched them and pulled out their hair, there's this lovely little sentence, 'From then on, they did not marry.' That is leadership. I was never trained in that in my theological college.

A friend of mine in a church in California had a woman who, almost every Sunday, walked past him, shook his hand and said something negative about the service. Every Sunday: 'Didn't enjoy that. Thought the second point wasn't very good. Didn't enjoy the hymns.' Every morning he would say 'Oh, I'm sorry, I'll think about that.' Then, one day, something snapped inside him and he said, 'Madam, one day I will bury you!' That is leadership. We need women and men of Deborah's courage to rise above the background that we find ourselves in, to be liberated from it and to do what God calls us to do.

- *What does it mean to be a courageous Christian leader today? What are the particular issues in the church and in society on which Christian leaders have to take a stand?*
- *When was the last time you were a courageous Christian, taking a stand on a particular moral or social issue?*

DO WHAT YOU CAN – NOT WHAT YOU CAN'T

Secondly, notice in the conversation with Barak Deborah does what she can do, but she doesn't do what she can't do. This is absolutely fundamental to all leadership. She leads, but she doesn't lead the troops into battle as the military commander. They probably wouldn't have followed a woman anyway. That would have been the final indignity. She is the spiritual, judging, visionary head of this cluster of tribes at the time. But she knows that she can't do it all and so she summons Barak who, wisely in my view, knows that Deborah's presence is a kind of guarantee of God's presence in the military episode. He wants to send a signal to the troops, not that they are being led by a woman, but that by the presence of a representative, the living God is going with them, and so victory is assured.

Part of the problem with leadership in our churches is we're not very courageous. We do our best at times simply to get through from one Sunday to another. Part of the problem in many of our churches is that we have appointed the wrong people to lead our churches. We are training loads of pastors, and they're good and godly people, but they're not leaders. The church desperately needs a way out of this morass in which we find ourselves. We need courage.

We also need those who recognise their limitations. There are many things I cannot do. Leaders who don't understand that end up either in burn-out or making stupid mistakes, because they do the whole thing themselves. We've got to learn where we're not gifted. If you're in leadership, God's calling you to do some things and to stop doing others. Your church is longing for you to stop doing some things. That will do two very special things: it will bless them no end and other people will rise up who can do those things as you mentor, train and release them. Deborah did what she could do, but not what she couldn't do.

- *Why do leaders and even regular members of the congregation feel that they need to 'do it all' in church ministry whether they're gifted or not?*
- *What can we learn from the experience of Moses and the apostles when they 'did what they could do and not what they couldn't do'? Look at Exodus 18:13-27 and Acts 6:1-7.*

LISTEN TO GOD

Thirdly, notice that Deborah heard from God. If I was asked to define the one characteristic of leadership we need in this third millennium it's this. We need men and women who hear from God. Notice in chapter 4:4, she is described not as a judge but as a prophetess. The other judges, or some of them at least, are not described in this way. She is described as a leader, a judge, and a prophetess. She hears from God. She tells Barak that this battle's success is guaranteed. Why? Because she thinks it's a good idea? Because she knows there is going to be a flash flood in the plain? Because she's already got it planned? No. Because she's heard from God. A.W Tozer made one of the most stark condemnations of perfunctory, ordinary Christian leadership. He said, 'The difference between the priest who has read and the prophet who has seen is as wide as the sea.' We dare not have our pulpits filled with people who are merely clever theologically, brilliant administratively, and attractive in the pulpit. We'd better have our leaders hearing from God. Part of the missing dimension of our churches is the prophetic insight that says, 'We believe that God is in this, and we will walk with him.'

When we talk about prophecy, I am not speaking about those one or two sentence contributions that sometimes come in the context of worship. They have their value, I am not being disparaging, but I am not speaking of them in this context. I am speaking about women and men who stride the mountains with power, who hear God's voice. This journey was undertaken by Job in his suffering. Right at the end of the book, agony after agony – the loss of family, of clothing, of sheep, of well-being, of livelihood, what happens? Job says this amazing sentence: 'I used to know you by the hearing of my ear, but now my eye sees you.'

Our churches will not be transformed by leadership that is simply keeping abreast of all the latest programmes that are coming out of the United States, or the latest book, or the latest bestseller or the latest courses. These things have their place but they are no substitute for leaders who hear from God. We desperately need to cry out for this authority in our lives, the willingness to go out on a limb for God, to hear his voice clearly and to respond to it. We need leaders who are into the Scripture, and into prayer, and into openness to the power of the Holy Spirit in their lives, and into submission to his will, and into seeing him as what matters more than anything else.

- *Why is listening to God often not a priority for leaders and other Christians? What pressures and temptations do we face?*

- *What difference did hearing from God make to Moses, Josiah and Paul? Look at Exodus 34:29, 2Kings 23:1-7, 21-25, Acts 16:6-10. What difference does it make when you take time to hear from God?*

CONCLUSION: THE LEADERS WE NEED

Deborah could easily have been crushed by the cabal of men that must have been around at the time, yet courage marks her leadership. She could have easily been arrogant, once she had established her position, and done everything. But she recognises the wisdom of letting Barak do his thing so she can do her thing and together they're far stronger than if they operated separately. Thirdly, she is a woman in touch with God, the source of power. It's great to be in touch with the source of power, the final authority. Prayer, reading the Bible, worship and so on – these things don't seem very much in themselves but they are access points into the power behind them. This ancient book, for all it was written two thousand years ago and more, is the access point into the power of the living God. Let's pray for an army of leaders to be raised up in our churches to affect our nation with the good news of Jesus, believing that our churches will be transformed by the kind of leaders we pray into place over these next few years.

- *Even if you don't consider yourself a leader, what have you learnt from Deborah's leadership?*

FURTHER STUDY

What is your view on the role of women in the church? Take time to look at the biblical evidence before you reach a conclusion. Look up passages such as 1 Corinthians 14:33-35 and 1Timothy 2:9-15 and consult concordances. How do these passages square with the account of Deborah in Judges 4 or Priscilla in Acts 18:24-26? If you want to do further research two accessible books which present opposing views are Wayne Grudem and John Piper's *Recovering Biblical Manhood and Womanhood*[3] and *Beyond Sex Roles*[4] by Gilbert Bilezikian. Or if they are hard to get hold of, try *Equal to Serve*[5] by Gretchen Gaebelein Hull.

REFLECTION AND RESPONSE

Whether you consider yourself to be leader or not, reflect on the extent to which you share Deborah's character qualities:

- Are you a courageous Christian standing up for God's priorities and values at home, at work, in the church and in the community?
- Do you know your limitations and the areas in which God has designed you to serve?
- Are you listening to God daily and willing to be obedient to his voice?

In twos, pray for your church leaders – not just your minister but those who lead the various ministries. Is there a practical way you could show your support for them this week?

During the week, take time out to listen to God. If you have a day off perhaps you could set aside a few hours or carve out time in the evening when the children are in bed. Pray, spend time reading the Bible and meditating on individual verses. Is there something God wants to say to you as an individual or as a family? Is there a specific task he has for you in the church or community?

If it is appropriate, share what God says to you with a prayer partner or another member of the group.

POINTS TO PONDER

- What have you learnt about God?
- What have you learnt about yourself?
- What actions or attitudes do you need to change as a result?

CHAPTER 14

David – A man after God's own heart

Aim: To appreciate the value of 'doing the right thing'

FOCUS ON THE THEME
Share examples of Christian leaders, politicians, media personalities, members of your congregation or friends who you consider 'did the right thing' in a particular situation even though their decision may not have been easy or popular. Why do they stand out to you? What do you admire about them and their choices?

Read: 2 Samuel 11:1 – 2:13

INTRODUCTION

Here we are at a very pivotal story in the Old Testament. I think it's pivotal for a number of reasons: it deals with David, who was described as a man after God's own heart; a terrible flaw in his character, his gross sins and then his period of recovery.

1) The fault line

Our society has a fault line in it, an opening through which Satan comes in and exploits our culture. My reading of world history is that all societies have various strengths and weaknesses. Modernity, the period up until about 1990, had certain flaws in it which the devil exploited. The church was trying to work out its faith in the context of scientific certainty, and so there was confidence in science, and Christianity was thought of as just faith. 'Christianity deals with faith, science deals with facts' – those were the kind of things we were told. When post-modernity hit town we realised that science was far from being infallible, and that science was actually based on something called presuppositions, which in Christian talk means faith, and that we weren't very sure about those presuppositions. So post-modernity has opportunities for the gospel and conflict for the church. Every age has things in the culture which provide opportunity, and things in the culture which provide threats. Don't be afraid of post-modernity; it's a strange new world for many of us but it does actually pose opportunities for the church as well as threats.

I believe societies are often vulnerable at particular points, and one of the points of vulnerability in our society is the area of sexuality. The devil is using that very issue to drive home his advantage in our culture. We have young people in their millions whose lives are being messed up because of this. And not just young people, older people too are having their lives deeply hurt because of an inadequate understanding of sexuality. The church is partly to blame. Certainly in the day I grew up, it hardly ever addressed the subject, and when it did, it addressed it with prudish reticence.

It is inappropriate to speak about certain aspects of sexual behaviour in a public setting such as this, and one wants to be careful about such intimate things. Nevertheless, the church will pay a heavy price if we do not tell our young people, particularly, what God's values are in the area of sexuality. If you've got a teenage child, let me tell you this, they are bombarded with more sexual images every day than you were every year. Our world has been sexualised dramatically. In that setting, we hear today a story of a man whose sexual appetite got him into enormous trouble and what he did to get out of it.

2) The characters

Let me give you some background to this passage. There are three characters we are going to look at, three interplays going on in this story. There is David, there's Uriah and there is Nathan the prophet. Bathsheba, actually, plays almost no role in the story. Bathsheba would have had no choice. At this period of history, her life would have been worth nothing had she resisted the king's advances.

Now let me trace some background for you in our Bible reading this morning, before we come to these three characters and the lessons to be learned from them. In the earlier part of the week, we were looking at those twelve or thirteen judges and they operated in a kind of two hundred year time frame. That little league of warring tribes were trying to bind together to become a nation state. Towards the end of the book Samuel arises, the overwhelmingly significant judge. We know about Samuel, his incredible birth and his miraculous early ministry. As Samuel goes on in his life and ministry the people of God are increasingly welded together as this nation state, and become jealous of surrounding nations, and cry out against Samuel and to God, 'Give us a king.' Against Samuel's better judgment, he anoints Saul, a giant of a man. Ultimately Saul dies, and David, having been anointed king some years earlier, ascends to the throne.

The reigns of David and Solomon, the second and third kings, are the high spot in Israelite history. They rule the united kingdom when the Philistines are largely suppressed. After Solomon, when Rehoboam and Jeroboam come along, the kingdom is divided and from then on there is dissension, failure and the Israelites fall away from God time and again. Some of them are taken into captivity in Babylon and are there for seventy years. When they return, Nehemiah and Ezra struggle to restore the nation in Jerusalem.

So in a sense, the high spot of the nation's fortunes is found here in Samuel, with David, a man after God's own heart. Samuel anoints David, he finds himself king, and here we are in Chapter 11 of 2 Samuel. Let me talk you through the passage, and then talk about these three characters.

3) A time for war

Look at verse 1 of Chapter 11: 'In the spring at the time when kings go off to war ...' There was a war season and there was a closed season in which there were training camps and people got new coaches in. Sometimes they went on occasional forays and tours to beat up people in nicer climates, and they regularly picked off the odd little tribe and beat them eight-one. But they wouldn't get into the main season until the spring rains had stopped. Iron chariots have become established now. They have moved from being hillside warriors, although David was good with a sling, into a much more sophisticated military machine. The kings went off to war when the rains had finished and it was possible for chariots to go over dry ground without sinking into the mud. So a truce seemed to be called each winter.

They were constantly fighting at this period of history. 'David sent Joab out with the king's men and the whole Israelite army. They destroyed the Ammonites and besieged Rabbah' – which is fifty miles east of Jerusalem. Fifty miles doesn't seem a long way away, but if you're walking there, weighed down in armour, it is. David remained in Jerusalem. In one sense this was not at all unusual. It was very common in the ancient world for the king to send out his chief military general to fight battles for him and then report back, and he would stay in the safety of the palace. However, there was a crack team of SAS Israelites, known as 'the kings' men'. There are David's crack troops, the king's men; and 'then the rest of the army'. The king would almost always lead the king's men, particularly as he'd gathered many of them together during his freelance fighting days as a mercenary, in the cave of Adullam. What on earth is he doing in Jerusalem? He should not have remained there. This is a dereliction of duty. He's in the wrong place. God could have said to David: 'What are you doing here, in your palace, when your men and the whole army are laying down their lives? You need to be offering spiritual leadership.'

4) The wrong place, the wrong time

'One evening David got up from his bed.' Actually, the Hebrew means the late afternoon. It looks like David had been lying on his bed long after the siesta; he was both in the wrong place and being lazy. We will come back to these things in a minute. 'From the roof he saw a woman bathing. The woman was very beautiful' and so on. This is not a routine bath. In fact she may not have bathed as we understand it at all, it may have been simply servants pouring water over her, but she is being made ceremonially clean. It may be that David, seeing this and realising that it was a ceremonial act signaling the end of her menstrual cycle, believed that she was in less danger of conceiving because of the particular period in the menstrual cycle in which he was going to engage in intercourse with her.

The story goes on and we see the attempt to con Uriah into believing that he ought to be with his wife, and he's a man who won't do that, so he's put in the hottest place of the battle. He's killed. The thing which David did displeases the Lord, and Nathan comes along with his prophetic insight and tells David a story. Nathan would consult David regularly, because Nathan was a prophet but David would also deal with judicial questions. It wouldn't be at all unusual for him to be consulted about the law of the land and its application, particularly in complex cases. So a story is told, David comes to genuine repentance, the child sadly dies, and David's dynasty moves on.

Now let me take you back to 2 Samuel 11 to look at these three characters and say something briefly about their three identities and their attributes. This really is an anatomy of lust. Lust, remember, is not simply a sexual thing, it is a desire to own or acquire that which is not yours. I think what's going on here in David is not so much sexual as an issue related to power and acquisition. David had more than one wife, he had any number of concubines, he could have slept with a whole range of women, which, in the culture of the day, would have been perfectly appropriate, but what does he do? He wants somebody else's wife. David is sexually inflamed, as a red-blooded man, but it is also a question of saying, 'I can have this, I want it, and so I will take it.' That wasn't unusual for eastern dictators, which is basically what David was, but it was unusual, the writer leads us to believe, in the case of a man after God's own heart. He was a pious man, who made a show of his spirituality, and not just a show, he really was hungry to know and do God's will. But he was in the wrong place and he was idle. Frankly, more people have fallen into sin because of the combination of those two things than almost any other. They're in the wrong place. What are you doing in the place of temptation?

What was David doing in bed halfway through the afternoon, bored, wondering how to fill his time? He should have been at the battlefront. There are three steps to falling into lust, and they are clear in this passage. David saw her; he sent for her, he slept with her. Those three phrases show the downward descent in this anatomy of lust.

Men down the ages, women too from time to time but specifically men, have trodden this downward path to their ruin. I believe the Holy Spirit wants this issue to be raised with the church. It is a devastating indictment on the church that people in pastoral leadership, ministers, vicars, elders, deacons, home group leaders, without number, have fallen into sexual sin in the last twenty to twenty-five years. This sin infects the church in a horrible way.

- *In what ways should the church address the subject of sexuality? How can it help young people in particular to 'do the right thing' regarding sexual morality?*
- *Why is 'being in the wrong place and being idle' usually a recipe for sin?*
- *Consider your own areas of weakness. What usually tempts you to sin? What usually marks the beginning of 'the downward descent' for you?*

5) The lust of the eyes

David sees this woman having water poured over her, and the Bible says she is a very beautiful woman. The Bible is not against sexuality. God is not against sex; he invented it.

Sexual expression within the context of marriage is a beautiful and wonderful thing. But we men, particularly, are driven by our eyes to see what we shouldn't see and let our minds dwell on it; we entertain it, and it can lead to action. That is why, for Christian men in their thousands, pornography is such a problem. Because we see something with our eyes and it's everywhere, we let our minds dwell on it, we send for it, as it were, we find opportunities to see it in other settings, and before we know where we are, our very soul is corrupted. It may lead to an adulterous act, it may not, but the seeds of sexual sin are sown in our lives. Most of us, as men, are dominated by what we see. He saw her. If he'd been in the bedroom and his servants had said, 'David, come on out, there's a woman on the roof having a shower,' I doubt whether he'd have been tempted. But because he went outside and saw her, with his own eyes ... That's a difference between men and women. It's important for us to see this downward path, and to remind ourselves of the awfulness of letting our eyes dwell on things they ought not to.

David could have stopped, wandered back into the house, he could have been sexually aroused, slept with one of his own wives, forgot the whole thing, taken a cold shower, anything. But he takes the next fatal step. He says, 'Who is she? Find out a little bit more.' You see, he's not sinning at the moment. How many men, particularly, have excused sin in their lives by simply entertaining it slightly? 'I'm not really quite sinning yet, just let me know a little bit more, just let my eyes linger a little bit longer.' It's not a sin for David to find out who she is. She's one of his subjects. It's a perfectly reasonable question at one level, 'Who is that woman?' But when she comes, he sleeps with her and she becomes pregnant. Watch what you watch, be careful about what you see and think about, because in the end you may do something horrific in the sexual arena.

Then notice how David follows this up with the most grotesque forms of deceit. He tries to get Uriah drunk, gets him back home, and Uriah simply refuses to give in. I don't suppose he suspected anything; he just didn't want to do what was wrong, and so David had him brutally killed. Nathan comes to him and rebukes him, and in the end David realises with stark horror what he has done.

One of the great things about this story is that the Bible doesn't seek to gloss over one of the great heroes of the faith. There is only one character in the whole Bible who lives perfectly from beginning to end, and it's Jesus. Every other character has a flaw of some kind. The Bible is not like many other religious writings, it doesn't gloss over the cracks of its heroes. It doesn't say 'They were all wonderful.' No, it tells us exactly the deceitfulness of the human heart.

It's not until David gets round to writing Psalm 51 that we discover the depth of his forgiveness. 'Have mercy on me, O God, for I know my transgression and my sin is ever before me. Create in me a pure heart, O God, renew a steadfast spirit within me. Do not cast me off from your presence. Restore to me the joy of my salvation.' 'That's the problem,' says David, 'I need to be pure inside, I need a pure heart.'

- *Scan 2 Samuel 11:1-15: at what points could David have halted his descent into sin? At what points could he have 'done the right thing'?*

6) Hope

There is a way back. The David who blatantly stole a fellow Israelite's wife, committed adultery with her and had her husband murdered, which makes him a liar, a murderer, a deceiver and an adulterer, that David who hit rock bottom in this episode, finds himself in Psalm 51 saying sorry to God and receiving forgiveness. We believe in a God who saves not just to the uttermost, but to the guttermost. And whoever we are, whatever the grossness of our sin, however far short of God we are, there is nothing so awful that you may have done that, if you are genuinely repentant, God can't forgive you. There is hope.

- *Read 2 Samuel 12:11-31. In what ways did David 'do the right thing' when Nathan confronted him with his sin? How would his response have been pleasing to God?*
- *What does Psalm 51 teach us about how to repent, about how to do 'the right thing' when we have sinned?*

7) Uriah the faithful

The other character in the story is Uriah. I really think he's going to be in God's hall of fame. What a man. He refuses to take advantage of his men, who are out there fighting. When he's sent back home he says, 'I'm not going to sleep with my wife and enjoy her company while my men are out there sleeping rough. It would be wholly inappropriate.' Faithful to his wife; faithful to his commanding officer, the king, even though the king was the very one who was deceiving him and cheating him; faithful to his men; faithful to his fellow officers; faithful to his values. I think Uriah is one of those unsung heroes because of his sheer dogged determination to be faithful. In the end it gets him killed. If he had compromised at any point, his life would have been spared. But because he refuses to compromise and he is faithful, he goes down in the hall of fame: Uriah the faithful.

There are people in our churches that are spectacularly gifted but they are here today and gone tomorrow. I've got people that I know, some of them have been linked with my own church, some of them will be in yours, who for months or even years seemed to be great youth leaders, brilliant deacons or fantastic elders, but they had no staying power; they forgot that the Christian life's not a sprint, it's a marathon. What's God calling us to? Faithfulness, day by day, dogged determination to do the right thing. Who went down in the Israelite history books? David. Who did the faithful thing? Uriah. Who gets all the praise in our churches? People with the spectacular gifts. Who will be in the hall of fame when you think of great Christians? William Carey, and Billy Graham and all those names. When God writes his history of planet Earth, there will be some names on that list you've never heard of, because they were the ones that kept the church going and kept the kingdom on track, because they were completely faithful in good times and bad.

8) Nathan

Nathan emerges from this story with enormous credit because he was not prepared to let power, influence, or possibly the threat of his own death deter him from doing the right thing. We need men and women like this to be raised up, who are not afraid of political correctness or cultural normality, inside or outside the church, but who are prophetic enough to hear God's voice and speak out words of truth.

Now there are dangers here. One is that some of us will say, 'Yes, I want to be a Nathan. I'm going to go back from this conference and I'm going to speak to my minister and I am going to confront every sign of weakness in our church.' That's not being prophetic. We've got to be careful. But we do need those who are prepared to speak the truth in love, and to confront evil even when it's found in high places, as well as low places. We must not behave with arrogant disregard for our leaders or anybody else, we've got to be sensitive and careful. Nevertheless, we have to be Nathan-like sometimes. Nathan was quite sensitive: he led David gently into his trap by telling him a story. I think that's really important, because before you can exercise the ministry of Nathan you have to realise that you are actually more like David. Only those people who have realised they're David can be Nathan in our churches. When you've come to that point, instead of pointing the finger at everybody in your church and saying, 'If only it wasn't for them, and them and them, this would be a great church. If only those people there would leave, this would be my kind of church', we'd better say to ourselves, 'I am the man, O God.' As Psalm 51 says, 'Against you, and you only, have I sinned. Forgive me LORD.'

As we go on receiving that forgiveness, recognising our own failings – we may not be guilty of adultery and murder but we have all offended a holy God and must come to him in humility for grace and forgiveness – may God give us Nathan's ability to confront sin and wrong where we find it in order to keep the church on track, and in order to see more and more Uriahs raised up among us. We need people who won't compromise their principles, who won't settle for comfort when principle is involved, who will do the right thing even if it costs them their lives. What a great story this ends up being. From a horrific denial of God's values, it ends in grace, forgiveness and cleansing. It ends in prophetic leadership of the Nathan style. It ends with a man who dies brutally and unjustly but at least he goes to God knowing this, he did the right thing. May that be written on all our gravestones, 'He did the right thing.'

- *Consider Nathan's manner and the content of what he said to the king. In what ways was he 'doing the right thing'?*

- *Why is 'doing the right thing', being faithful and confronting sin in the church and society, often an unpopular choice among Christians?*
- *What are the rewards and motivation for 'doing the right thing'? For some examples look at Matthew 25:14-30; 2 Timothy 2:4-6, 3:12-15, 4:6-8; Hebrews 12:1-3.*

FURTHER STUDY

Scan through 1 Samuel 16 to 1 Kings 2:12 which covers the period from David's anointing as king to his death. Despite David's sins and many failures, why do you think he was called 'a man after God's own heart'? (1 Sam. 13:14) Why do you think David merited this title but not his predecessor Saul? And what does this title tell us about God's values and priorities? How can we be men and women after God's heart?

REFLECTION AND RESPONSE

In what area of your life do you need to 'do the right thing'?

- Are you like David – do you need to repent for a particular sin? If so meditate on Psalm 51 and spend time in silent confession.
- Are you like Uriah – is God asking you to be faithful to him in a particular area, even though it may go unnoticed by others and cost you dearly? Ask another member of the group to pray with you for God's strength regarding this issue.
- Are you like Nathan – is God asking you to confront sin and wrong within the Christian community? If it is appropriate, ask another member of the group or the home group leaders to pray with you for wisdom and sensitivity in this matter.

As a group thank God for his grace and forgiveness in our lives. He did not settle with 'doing the right thing' in regard to our sin, he did not deal with us as we deserved, but in his grace and kindness sent

Jesus to die in our place. If it is appropriate, share communion together, remembering God's tremendous grace towards us, not just at Calvary but every day that we live.

POINTS TO PONDER

- What have you learnt about God?
- What have you learnt about yourself?
- What actions or attitudes do you need to change as a result?

CHAPTER 15

Joshua – The crossover man

Aim: To learn how to deal with changes in society and in the church

FOCUS ON THE THEME
What is the biggest change you have had to cope with in recent months – it may have been at work, in your relationships, in your home or at church. What strategies did you use to cope with this change? On a scale of 1-5 (1 being poor and 5 being great) rate how well you dealt with the new challenge.

Read: Joshua 1:1-9

INTRODUCTION

Our Bible character today is the character of Joshua. He may have been about eighty years of age here. This incident takes place between twelve hundred and fourteen hundred years before Jesus was born. Joshua is a crossover man. In Joshua 3 we read the story of him crossing over from one side of the Jordan to the other, as a sign that the Israelites have finished wilderness wandering and are now on the way to becoming a settled people in a land which God has given them.

Throughout the Bible there are significant characters that straddle very significant shifts in culture. Joshua takes the Israelites from that wilderness wandering into the beginning of establishing the tribes being bonded together and sets the scene for the thirteen judges who are to follow. The ultimate crossover man is Jesus Christ, the God-man who crossed over from AD to BC, and the whole new model for relating to God through his death is established in his person. Jesus stands astride this great cosmic change.

I think that we are on the cusp of a major change in our culture, and the change from modernity to post-modernity is so significant, we will never go back to the way things were. We might go on to better things, we might go on to worse things, but we are in a very significant crossover time. The battle for the heart and soul of our nation is on.

- *What do you think have been the most significant changes in our society in the last twenty years?*
- *What new opportunities do these changes provide for spreading the gospel? Be specific.*

It is interesting that the word 'Joshua' is the Old Testament equivalent of the name 'Jesus'. Why is Jesus called Jesus? Matthew 1:21 says: 'You are to give him the name Jesus, because he will save his people from their sins.' Joshua is the Old Testament equivalent. The book of Joshua sets out the story of that great deliverance from wilderness wandering to the Promised Land. Some people have thought that Canaan was a kind of metaphor for crossing the Jordan and going into heaven. Now I don't think the Old Testament writers ever expected us to understand Canaan as heaven. I think they expected us to see it as a metaphor for the Christian life, with all its troubles and traumas, but never for heaven.

In Joshua 1, 2 and 3, you see the Israelites on the verge of Jordan. Jericho is conquered once they've crossed the Jordan, and the whole of the book of Joshua is this great story of conquering the Promised Land and getting it established for God and his people. In Chapter 1 you've got the background. Joshua is just the man they need to take them from being pioneers to being settlers. What will it mean? How will they be governed? How will they be led? Who will hold them together? Joshua is our man. Let's look at some of the struggles he faced and at some of the lessons we can learn.

1) Moses is dead

Joshua 1 verse 1: 'After the death of Moses the servant of the LORD, the LORD said to Joshua son of Nun, Moses' assistant; "Moses my servant is dead."' Now you may not think that's very profound, but actually the book starts in a place which is absolutely essential to understanding Joshua's leadership role. 'Moses is dead.' The end of the old way is here. For forty years and more Moses had led the people of God, through thick and thicker, through bad and worse, and occasionally good. He was a fabulous leader. Moses was a tough act to follow. He was brilliant. Everybody spoke well about Moses: They don't speak about you like that when you're alive, but when you're dead, they say you're great. The way to be loved in your own church, particularly if you're the pastor, is to be the pastor who was the one before the pastor who is there now.

Moses is dead. But make no mistake, Moses was profoundly influential on the whole structure and nature of the people of God. Who would follow a man like Moses, for goodness sake? They'd seen him in operation. The older ones had seen him, the whole plagues business, crossing the Red Sea, the pillars of fire and cloud. 'Moses – what a leader!' But I have to tell you this; Moses was the wrong man to take the children of Israel to the next phase. We are in enormous danger when we do more than honour the past. We should always honour it but we must never live in it.

We are in crossover time in this new millennium. We need men and women to be raised up who honour the past, who draw on its lessons with wisdom, but who dare not live in that past. These are new days. We look back to the great heroes of the saints who were absolutely fantastic. They're dead, and we do not honour their memory by living with their structures or their expressions of truth. Moses was dead. The old way was finished, the new way was beginning. But two things were going to keep Joshua and two things are going to keep us in this world. We're going to have Moses' God and Moses' book. We're not going to have Moses. That's absolutely essential. Some of us are so incredibly locked in the past that we cannot see the new thing God wants to do. Do you see the difference? It's important, it's essential that we understand this difference between tradition and traditionalism. Tradition is a marvellous thing. Traditionalism is a terrible thing. Tradition is the living faith of the dead. Traditionalism is the dead faith of the living. Those two things are poles apart. We honour our past. We thank God for Moses. But he's dead. Now move on.

- *Consider your own church practices. In what ways might you be in danger of living in the past? In these specific areas what would it mean to honour the past rather than live in it?*

2) Facing change

I know, as we get older, facing change is difficult. That's one of the reasons why the whole generation had to die out in the wilderness, because Joshua needed a new generation to move into this new land. I pray constantly to God, 'Dear God, do not let me be passed over, for you to bless somebody else because I am resistant to the things you want to do.' The enormous danger is that I know how to preach, to break bread and serve wine, to baptise people, to visit the sick, and I just go on doing those things as if nothing ever changes. There's a world out there that's dying without Jesus. We need new models of leadership, new paradigms for the way we have to operate.

- *What role can older believers have in facilitating change in the church rather than hindering it?*
- *How would you respond to an older Christian who said 'Today we have change in the church for change's sake. Young people want to avoid establishing traditions, unfortunately mistaking substance and ritual for traditionalism.'*

3) Have a big vision

Joshua, son of Nun, is about to rise up. 'Now then, you and all these people, get ready to cross the Jordan.' I don't know how many there were, hundreds of thousands. Crossing the Jordan at this point is a terribly difficult and dangerous task. The Jordan is narrow, pulsating and fast. The slopes are steep and crumbly and at any moment people could be rushed down into the torrent to their death. '... get ready to cross the Jordan River into the land I am about to give to them – to the Israelites. I will give you every place where you set your foot, as I promised Moses.' 'Every place you set your foot' – do you remember where that's going to be? Lebanon in the north, the Euphrates in the south and the east and the great Mediterranean Sea in the west: 'Every place you set your foot will be yours.' Joshua marched in with a big vision.

What do you want to accomplish? Have you noticed that many of us have got such small visions and small ambitions? God calls us to a massive, enormous, macro-vision of what he wants us to do, as house-group leaders, as pastors, as Sunday-school teachers, to lift our eyes above the ordinary.

4) God with us

The God of Moses was with him. 'No one will be able to stand up against you,' verse 5, 'all the days of your life.' Was God with Moses? Absolutely. 'As I was with Moses, so I will be with you; I will never leave you nor forsake you.' Hopefully we have big dreams and big plans, wanting God to be at work in our churches, our home groups, and we are not alone. Isn't it comforting to have a human person with us at times when we're insecure? We've got more than a person with us. God promises, as he was with Joshua, to be with us. The Holy Spirit is here, and he's in us and loves us and wants to go with us. There's no place on earth God's presence can't go with you. He's with you by the power of the Spirit. You are not alone.

Joshua goes to conquer unknown territory because Moses' God is with him. Moses wasn't there. That was a terribly insecure feeling for Joshua. He had spent forty years observing the great man at work. People ape and copy what they see. Many older folk have got an enormous responsibility in your church. You are watched by younger people and younger Christians.

Joshua didn't just look at Moses for a week and think, 'Oh, I'm going to copy that.' He'd eaten with him, watched as Jethro had told him off for coping with too many people, seen him struggle with speaking to a rock and hitting a rock and pleasing God and offending God, and getting it wrong and getting it right. He'd seen Moses through all those struggles, and his hand-holding mentor is gone. That feels bad. So God said to Joshua, 'Moses may be dead, your human support is absent, but I, who was with Moses all the time you were watching him, I will also be with you.' It's the same God, and he needed to know that.

5) Obey my word

Also, he had Moses' book. Verse 8: 'Do not let this Book of the Law depart from your mouth.' Keep on speaking about it, think about it and then be careful to do it. God is saying to Joshua, 'I know you're feeling insecure, but you will have two things Moses had: me and Moses' book.' We have Moses' God by the power of the Spirit, and we have all sixty-six books of the Bible. But notice that Joshua is not simply to affirm it and to honour it, but to be careful to do everything written in it.

We say this is God's holy and inspired word. We treasure it. The danger is that somehow we honour these pages, but that's not what Joshua's being commanded to do. Don't take the scrolls around and set them up on your mantelpiece and bow to them a few times. Evangelicals have been terribly guilty of this. We keep saying, 'It's the word, it's the Bible, that's what's important.' How many of us are reading it regularly and obeying its teaching? That's the point of the Scripture. It is so important that we do what the book says.

My wife is going through a phase of life, some mid-life crisis. She's going systematically through our house throwing things out, painting things, changing the kids' rooms around. She buys one of the girls a wardrobe. The other wardrobe seems to me to be perfectly good, but apparently it's not quite the right shape, and now they're older they have more things that hang like this and not like this. It gets delivered to the house, and I come home late, you know, wanting her to have a ribbon in her hair ... she says, 'Oh, darling' in her best Delilah voice 'we need to put this together tonight.' I am useless, practically. I have to have a week of prayer and fasting to change a light bulb. So she says, 'I'll help.'

We read the instructions. Have you ever read those instructions? You have to have a degree in engineering just to understand what 'Tab A' means. Then the phone rings and it's somebody from her family in America, and she's on the phone for three hours – and she leaves me upstairs. I think, 'This is ridiculous, any idiot should be able to do this.' So I hammer a nail into this thing. Then she comes back, aghast. She says, 'What have you done with those two bits? You didn't read the instructions, did you, while I was gone?' She gets all sort of ... female. And I say, 'Yes, I did,' and then she says, 'No you didn't', and we have this great war, and then eventually I say, 'No, all right, I didn't but it looked all right.' We go downstairs, we get the pliers and pull the nail out and she's right all along, I hadn't read the blessed instructions, the wardrobe's never going to get done tonight and our poor daughter will die without a wardrobe, obviously.

Anyway, I had to take it all apart, because I hadn't read the instructions. It was a complete disaster. In the end we sat up half the night and did this wretched wardrobe. Apparently it's fixed and apparently our daughter's thrilled, and apparently I've gone up in her estimation and my wife is still speaking to me. So it worked in the end. But I made a big mistake. I didn't obey the instructions.

We've laughed about a wardrobe, but every day of my life I see the wreckage of Christian lives of people who do not obey the instructions. If our world, ethically, economically, medically, politically and socially obeyed this book you would not believe the kind of world we would live in, Every day I meet people whose lives are damaged. They are so broken, so grotesquely disfigured by sin, because they have not obeyed the law that is God's holy and powerful word. 'Don't let it depart out of your mouth. Be careful to do everything I have written in it.'

- *When we have to negotiate change in our personal lives and in the church, what help do we have? What parts of the Bible have helped you cope with change in the past?*

6) Be strong and courageous

This section is topped and tailed with a little phrase God repeats twice, and it's particularly strong in the Hebrew. God says this, verse 6, 'Be strong and courageous.' And again in verse 9: 'Have I not commanded you? Be strong and courageous.' God tops and tails this promise by telling Joshua to be strong and courageous. I wonder what you would feel like if someone told you to be courageous. At first sight it seems a funny thing. We assume that being strong and courageous is something to do with our emotions. A problem comes along, and people seem to ride over it, and we think they are courageous. We imagine it's a feeling. Bravery, my friends, is not a feeling, it's a decision. It's going back and saying, 'Though my knees knock and my heart beats and races, though I sweat profusely, though I am anxious, I am going to go back and do what God wants me to do.' It's a decision. Of course, you need the power of the Spirit to do that. Joshua needed God with him; he couldn't have done it on his own, but it was a decision. That's why God could command it. If it's a feeling, not even God could command it. God can't say to you to feel something because we can't drum up a feeling. But we can drum up an activity, a decision, an act of the will. We can do it. What Joshua was being called to do was, 'Joshua, you'll face things that make your knees knock, but when they do, do it anyway.' Brave people are just as terrified as the rest of us, but they're braver for a second longer.

Wellington, the great military hero, is famous for being nervous before battles. He once was so nervous, his knees were shaking so much, that his attendants on either side had to hold him up while he was trying to get on his horse. His knees were physically shaking, and at the top of his voice he spoke to his knees. He said, 'Knees, you may shake how you will, and you'd shake even more if you knew where I was going to take you.' That's a decision. It's nothing to do with a feeling. If he'd let his feelings dominate him, he'd have gone back into the tent, had a cup of tea and sent the generals off to war. He decided to do the right thing. This is what Joshua is being asked to do, to make a decision, which was courageous, wise and strong. It's not a feeling. He probably felt terrified. 'Moses has gone and I cannot begin to imagine what awaits me.'

7) Follow the ark

That brings us neatly to Joshua 3. Joshua, having spied out Jericho, now feels he is able to take it, because of Rahab's careful insights. Notice two things for the people of God. Joshua 3:3: 'When you see the ark of the covenant of the LORD your God, and the priests who are Levites carrying it, you are to move out from your positions and follow it. Then you will know which way to go, since you have never been this way before.' What a definition of my life. I have never been this way before. Then it says, 'Keep a distance of about one thousand yards between you and the ark, don't go near it.' It may have been because the ark was holy, but I think there's a more pragmatic reason. I think that with a crowd of a hundred thousand plus, you need to stand away from it in order that everybody can see it, because you want them all to follow the ark.

All sorts of trends are going to come into the life of the church, programmes, plans, all sorts of biblical emphases.

Follow the ark of the covenant. Keep focused on Jesus. We can focus on the ark, the very presence of Jesus, which for us is the critical factor. Focus on him. There will be distractions; there will be things which take us off from one side to the other. Some of you who are older must feel that life is spinning so fast, you've no idea how you are going to cope. All the new developments, new technology, the new changes, and you come to church and you think, 'Thank you God, at least nothing changes here.' And blow me, they go and change things! The way some Christians talk about modern technology, you'd think God was surprised by the whole thing. I want to tell you, there's more power in the cross than in every single piece of technology you will ever discover. Watch the ark. Keep looking at Jesus; don't take your eyes off him. Follow your leaders in your church, praise God for them, pray for them, support them. They too want to follow Jesus, but keep your eyes on Jesus.

They got across the Jordan in ranks probably of five or six across, tightly packed in because I suspect that the place of crossing was narrow. It may have taken them hours to all get across, but they got there safely. Keep your eyes fixed on a fixed point. I'll tell you this. Your world may go mad, your job may change, technology may go berserk, morals may fall and slip, our nation may have a long way yet to go on its pathway towards hell. You think things are bad now, they may get much worse. They may not, please God. May we see revival in our land! But whatever happens, don't take your eyes off Jesus. He's not surprised by what is going on, he isn't fooled by it and guess what, more than anything he isn't threatened by it. He is all-powerful.

- *Look at Colossians 3:1-17. How can Christians keep focused on Jesus in a constantly changing world? What practical measures does Paul outline?*

8) God will do amazing things

Finally, Joshua told the people, verse 5, 'Consecrate yourselves, for tomorrow the LORD will do amazing things among you.' What a promise. Get through this, across the Jordan, and tomorrow God will do amazing things. Oh God, please raise up Joshuas who see this. Raise up people who are utterly devoted to this book, who are not prepared to compromise any bit of it at any point. Raise up people who are desperate for the power of God in their lives, who keep their eye on the Ark and who consecrate themselves so much to God that he can say, 'Tomorrow I'm going to do amazing things among you.'

I believe that many of those amazing things will take place here on earth. I believe that in the next few years, in our own country, some things will get very much worse and some things will get very much better. My prayer is that we will be part of churches that are going to make profound differences in our society. All the major political parties cannot see a way forward for our society in decay, apart from organisations that they call 'faith-based organisations'. We have a fabulous window of opportunity for amazing things in our communities. We need women and men of vision to consecrate themselves and to see those amazing things take place. There is coming a tomorrow when there will be an absolutely amazing thing, to top all amazing things, to beat even global revival, and that tomorrow will see every tear wiped away from your eyes. It will see every pain ended and every disease gone and every imperfection finished, and us in heaven with God for ever and ever, enjoying his presence in the amazing beauty of who he is. Consecrate yourselves today for tomorrow, literally, miracles may occur in your lives and your churches.

- *What will stop you seeing and being part of the changes that God has in store for this generation? Be specific.*

- *How does the hope of heaven and the promise of Christ's return help us deal with the changes we face in the church and in the world?*

FURTHER STUDY

Daniel was another Old Testament character who had to deal with radical change. He was one of the Israelites taken into exile in Babylon. This meant getting used to a new country, language, culture, laws and lifestyle. Read Daniel chapters 1-6. How did Daniel cope with this upheaval? What were the key factors in his ability to stay faithful to God in this new situation? What does Daniel's response and his experience of God in the midst of such uncertainty teach us?

REFLECTION AND RESPONSE

What changes or challenges are you facing now? How would you like to deal with them? What have you learnt from the study of Joshua which could help you? Bring your concerns and requests to God.

As a group, consecrate yourselves to God. This may involve a silent time of repentance; prayer for each other that God would help you stay pure and focused on him; space to think through your priorities to make room for daily devotions; a time of worship expressing your love for God.

Believe in God's promise to Joshua, 'Consecrate yourselves, for tomorrow the LORD will do amazing things among you.' Who knows what the Lord will do in you and through you as a result of spending time getting to know him through these studies!

REVIEW OF CHAPTERS 1-5

Each of the Old Testament characters we have looked at were flawed heroes. The Bible records for us their faithfulness and their failings, their obedience and their disobedience, their spiritual highs and their lows. Their imperfections encourage us that God uses individuals like us to fulfil his purpose but also to point us forward to Christ – the perfect Prophet, Judge and King; the one we really need to rule over us, guide us and lead us.

Reflect on what you have learnt from the lives of Elijah, Samson, Deborah, David and Joshua:

- If you are a leader, what have you learnt to help you in your role?
- How has your personal devotional life been challenged?
- What practical steps will you take to ensure your sexual purity?
- How will you reprioritise your time so that you can hear from God?
- What have you learnt about the exercise of power and authority?
- How have you been challenged about living in the past, resting in the present and dealing with the future?

If it is appropriate, pray through with another group what God has been teaching you. Discuss together how, with God's help, you have applied these truths to your life.

POINTS TO PONDER

- What have you learnt about God?
- What have you learnt about yourself?
- What actions or attitudes do you need to change as a result?

---

[1] F F Bruce, *In retrospect*, (Zondervan, 1993)
[2] John R W Stott and Timothy Dudley-Smith, Ed., *Authentic Christianity*, (Leicester: IVP, 1995)
[3] J Piper and W Grudem, *Recovering biblical manhood and womanhood: a response to evangelical feminism*, (Crossway books, 1992)
[4] G Bilezikian, *Beyond Sex Roles*, (Baker Book House, 1985)
[5] G G Hull, *Equal to Serve*, (Baker Book House, 1998)